LOS ANGELES

from the days of the Pueblo

List of Publications

Fabulous San Simeon, by Oscar Lewis. Illustrated with many beautiful photographs by Philip Negus Frasse. Paper, $1.50.

Los Angeles from the days of the Pueblo, by W. W. Robinson. Illustrated with many old and modern pictures, five in full color, plus map. Paper, $1.50; cloth, $4.00.

In preparation:

Columbia, Gem of the Southern Mines, by H. T. Rensch

Sutter's Fort and Old Sacramento, by Carroll Hall

Coloma and the Discovery of Gold, by Aubrey Neasham

Exclusive Distributor

LANE PUBLISHING CO.

Publishers of Sunset Magazine and Books
Menlo Park, California

Society members should order directly from the Society.
California purchasers must add four per cent sales tax.

Los Angeles

from the days of the Pueblo

TOGETHER WITH A GUIDE

TO THE HISTORIC

OLD PLAZA AREA

INCLUDING THE

PUEBLO DE LOS ANGELES

STATE HISTORICAL MONUMENT

By W. W. ROBINSON

Published by the

CALIFORNIA HISTORICAL SOCIETY

Acknowledgment

In the preparation of this book the author has had the active cooperation of the Division of Beaches and Parks of the Department of Natural Resources, State of California—under the jurisdiction of which "Pueblo de Los Angeles State Historical Monument" has been placed. Full cooperation, too, has been given by the Department of Recreation and Parks of the City of Los Angeles which (by agreement) represents both the City and the County of Los Angeles in this historical monument; and by the officers and directors of El Pueblo de Los Angeles, Inc. Acknowledgment is made, too, of the help given by the California Historical Society, through its staff and its publication committee. Specific thanks are due George L. Harding, Edwin H. Carpenter, Jr., Susanna Bryant Dakin, Allan Sproul, Aubrey Neasham, Mrs. Jean Martin, Glenn W. Price, Wendell Davis, David Y. Leach, Christine Sterling, and Mario Valadez. Ana Begué de Packman, steeped in Pueblo lore, has been helpful. For permission to reproduce on the front cover James Walker's painting "The Patrón" thanks are due Mrs. Reginald Walker of Oakland. Picture credits are given throughout the book, but the author is particularly grateful to Bettilee Byars, curator of the Historical Collection, Title Insurance and Trust Company; Frank B. Putnam, Historian, Security-First National Bank of Los Angeles; and Ruth I. Mahood, senior curator of history, Los Angeles County Museum. The figure of the early California musician reproduced on the half-title page is the work of Diana Bovee, done for the Museum. A special indebtedness is acknowledged to the author's wife, Irene Robinson.

COPYRIGHT 1959
CALIFORNIA HISTORICAL SOCIETY
2090 JACKSON STREET · SAN FRANCISCO, CALIFORNIA

LIBRARY OF CONGRESS
CATALOG CARD No. 59-12345

DESIGNED BY LAWTON KENNEDY

LITHOGRAPHED BY
HOOPER PRINTING & LITHOGRAPH COMPANY

I

Where Los Angeles Began

✿✿✿✿✿✿✿✿✿✿✿✿✿✿✿✿✿✿✿✿✿✿✿✿

 ON THE EVENING OF SEPTEMBER 4, 1781, the founders of Los Angeles—a group of weary men, women, and children—were camped on the west bank of a river in Southern California called then the Porciúncula.

These first settlers, forty-four in all, colonists from Mexico, were on a site chosen for a pueblo by Felipe de Neve, California's Spanish governor, because of the "fertility of the soil" and the "abundance of water for irrigation." With them, also, were the four soldiers who had been their escort that day from Mission San Gabriel and who would stay with them for a long time.

After a hot day of travel and toil, settlers and soldiers were gratefully aware of the slight coolness that came with dusk. The settlers—the "pobladores," they were called—were thankful to have reached their long-looked-for home after a thousand-mile journey that had its start early in the year in the Sinaloa and Sonora areas of Mexico. There these hardy people had been recruited to establish a farming community on this very river, later to be called the Los Angeles River. The products of their farms would help relieve young California's dependence on ship-borne importations of grain from far away San Blas. As they shared their tortillas and beans that first evening, we can well believe they talked of the snug adobe homes, the good stock, and the produce of the fields that soon would be theirs.

The site of the first plaza of this pueblo was the birthplace of Los Angeles. It was a parallelogram that lay just northwest of the present-day Plaza. Today it is the center of the "Pueblo de Los Angeles State Historical Monument"—sometimes called, for brevity's sake, the Plaza Project.

This state monument, part of the state's park system, had its origin in the minds of historically-inclined and community-conscious people. The idea was expressed in an agreement entered into in 1953 by the state, the county, and the city. Under its terms approximately ten square blocks of land, all within the old Pueblo area and including the heart of Spanish and Mexican Los Angeles, are being acquired by the state. This is done through purchase and condemnation, with funds contributed jointly by the state and by the county and city.

The development of this historical monument or park— under a master plan—preserves and recreates something of Los Angeles' Pueblo days. It helps interpret the story of the founding, growth, and evolution of Los Angeles. It keeps fresh in the minds of today's citizens the simple beginning of a city that through the succeeding years has stretched its limits to the south, the west, the east, and the north, filling valleys and spreading over hills, even touching the ocean twenty miles from the first plaza.

The sculptured figure of Father Junípero Serra, founder of the California missions, faces the Plaza from the east side. It stands on land that was the site of the capacious adobe home of Don Ygnacio del Valle. *Courtesy N. S. Di Palma, Los Angeles.*

Adjoining the state historical monument on the south and southwest are two other mighty developments in the making: the Civic Center and Bunker Hill. The Civic Center plan is again a state, county, and city effort, while the redevelopment of Bunker Hill into a towering, residential, business, and shopping center is a city and a federal affair. The three projects arise as a unit on several hundred acres of former Pueblo land. Monumental and breathtaking in scope, they transform a substandard region into a thing of interest, utility, and beauty. At the same time they create a thrilling center, close to the intersections of the Hollywood, the Harbor, and the Pasadena freeways, for a city that until recently has been a series of sprawling suburbs without an apparent heart. In developing these projects Los Angeles discovers that its original Spanish and Mexican Pueblo center coincides essentially with the administrative center of today's metropolitan area. Here Los Angeles becomes aware of its past, of the accomplishments of its present, and of the possibilities of its future.

Shrine on veranda of Ávila House. It was the Ávila House, temporary headquarters of Stockton in 1847, that inspired the reactivation of Olvera Street and gave stimulus to the Plaza Project. *Photo by Jack Sheedy: Vanguard.*

[7]

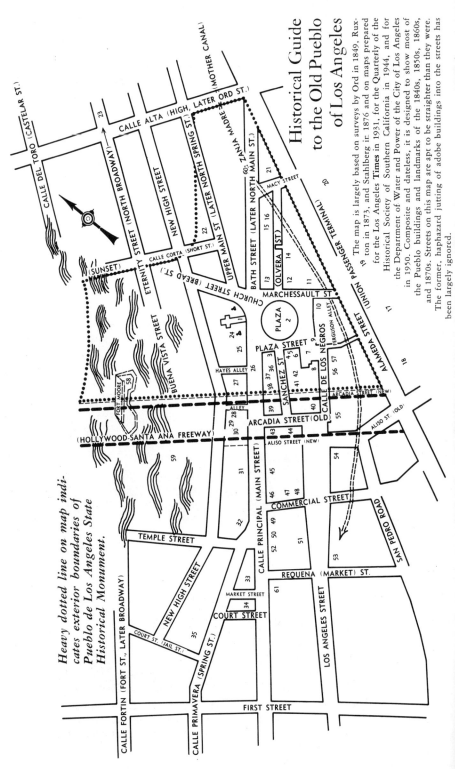

Historical Guide
to the Old Pueblo
of Los Angeles

The map is largely based on surveys by Ord in 1849, Ruxton in 1873, and Stahlberg jr. 1876 and on maps prepared for the Los Angeles *Times* in 1931, for the Quarterly of the Historical Society of Southern California in 1944, and for the Department of Water and Power of the City of Los Angeles in 1950. Composite and dateless, it is designed to show most of the Pueblo buildings and landmarks of the 1840s, 1850s, 1860s, and 1870s. Streets on this map are apt to be straighter than they were. The former, haphazard jutting of adobe buildings into the streets has been largely ignored.

Heavy dotted line on map indicates exterior boundaries of Pueblo de Los Angeles State Historical Monument.

CALLE DEL TORO (CASTELAR ST.)

CALLE ALTA (HIGH, LATER ORD ST.)

ETERNITY STREET (NORTH BROADWAY)

NEW HIGH STREET

CALLE CORTA (SHORT ST.)

UPPER MAIN ST. (LATER NORTH SPRING ST.)

60: ZANJA MADRE (MOTHER CANAL)

BATH STREET (LATER NORTH MAIN ST.)

MACY STREET

OLVERA ST.

CHURCH STREET (BREAD ST.)

MARCHESSAULT ST

(UNION PASSENGER TERMINAL)

ALAMEDA STREET

(SUNSET)

PLAZA
2

PLAZA STREET

CALLE DE LOS NEGROS

FERGUSON ALLEY

HAYES ALLEY

SANCHEZ ST.

ARCADIA STREET (NEW)

FORT MOORE

BUENA VISTA STREET

ALLEY

ARCADIA STREET (OLD)

ALISO ST. (OLD)

(HOLLYWOOD-SANTA ANA FREEWAY)

ALISO STREET (NEW)

COMMERCIAL STREET

SAN PEDRO ROAD

CALLE PRINCIPAL (MAIN STREET)

TEMPLE STREET

REQUENA (MARKET) ST.

MARKET STREET

COURT STREET

NEW HIGH STREET

LOS ANGELES STREET

COURT ST. (JAIL ST.)

CALLE FORTIN (FORT ST., LATER BROADWAY)

CALLE PRIMAVERA (SPRING ST.)

FIRST STREET

1. Plaza Church, started in 1818, dedicated in 1822.

2. Plaza, dating from 1818. (The earlier, original Plaza, dating from 1781, with its surrounding house-lots, guardhouse, officers' building, and granary, was northeast of the present Plaza Church.)

3. Pico House, dating from 1869, built on site of home of José Antonio Carrillo.

4. Pío Pico's townhouse (originally adjoining Carrillo's home.)

5. Home, at one time, of Andrés Pico, Pío's brother.

6. Fire House (1880s, 1890s).

7. Plazuela or "O'Campo's Plaza," cock-fighting center.

8. Francisco O'Campo's home (formerly that of J. B. Leandré).

9. Ignacio del Valle's townhouse. Today its site is a small park dominated by a statue of Junípero Serra.

10. Vicente Lugo's townhouse; later St. Vincent's College, predecessor of Loyola University. Today its site is a small park.

11. Juan Sepúlveda's townhouse.

12. Judge Agustín Olvera's home (originally that of Tiburcio Tapia); today site of Latin-American Hospitality Center Building.

13. Gambling house of Pedro Seguro in 1840s. (This adobe was later the Jones-Simpson home; its site now is Bank of America.)

14. Ávila House. (Originally it adjoined the Olvera house and had an elbow that extended nearly across present Olvera St.)

15. Sepúlveda House (standing on site of earlier adobe structures); now one of the larger adobe shops of Olvera Street.

16. Pelanconi Building (standing on site of earlier adobe structures), formerly home and wine-cellar of vintner Antonio Pelanconi; now La Golondrina Restaurant.

17. Old Chinatown, site of present Union Passenger Terminal.

18. Mateo Keller's Winery.

19. Juan Ramírez' home.

20. Benjamin D. Wilson's townhouse; later school and orphanage of Sisters of Charity.

21. Dr. Obed Macy's home.

22. José Mascarel's home.

23. The road to Campo Santo.

24. Early day cemetery adjoining Church on south.

25. Home of Doña Benancia Sotelo de Domínguez (originally built and owned by Carlos Baric), later Andrés Pico's townhouse. The adobe to the south was also Domínguez property.

26. Hayes Alley (also known as Bridge Street; as Republic Street; and as Turner Street).

27. Judge Benjamin Hayes' home (Served as courtroom.)

28. Montgomery Saloon.

29. M. Luis Bauchet's home.

30. Salazar Adobe. (Part used for postoffice).

31. Eulogio de Celis' townhouse; later site of Lafayette Hotel, afterward known as St. Elmo Hotel.

32. John Temple's store; later site of Downey Block, then U. S. Post Office.

33. Temple Block, built by John Temple as a two-story adobe in 1851-2; torn down to make room for three-story brick building —which, in turn, gave way to present City Hall.

34. City market, built by John Temple in 1859; upper story a theater. (Later used as Courthouse until torn down to make way for Bullard Block.)

35. José Antonio Rocha's townhouse—later used by city and county for council meetings and courtroom. A jail was built in rear.

36. Merced Theater, next to Pico House. (On its site stood originally the El Dorado Saloon, later to become Methodist Church.)

37. Masonic Lodge or Temple, built in 1858.

38. Sanchez Hall, originally — presumably — the Juzgado or Hall of Sessions.

39. Bell's Block, two-story frame building; first floor was Dr. A. W. Hope's pharmacy; second floor the home of Captain Alexander Bell.

40. Ignacio Coronel's home, used also as school and for theatricals.

41. Vicente Sanchez' two-story townhouse. (At a later date the Garnier Building arose near by, for half a century headquarters of the Chinese community.)

42. Francisco Sepúlveda's townhouse.

43. El Palacio, adobe mansion of Abel Stearns. (On its site stood earlier the home of Claudio Lopez, great-great-grandfather of Sheriff Eugene W. Biscailuz.) El Palacio gave way to the Baker Block, which in turn yielded to the Hollywood Freeway.

44. Arcadia Block.

45. Bella Union Hotel. (Built in 1835 by Isaac Williams for a store, it served as headquarters for Governor Pío Pico in 1845-6 and for Archibald Gillespie in 1846. Its site was the probable approximate location of Indian village of Yang-na.)

46. Charles Duccommun, jewelry and hardware. (Starting on Commercial Street, Duccommun expanded, taking in the general store at the corner on Main Street and extending to the Bella Union.)

47. Mateo Keller's store (merchandise and wine).

48. McFarland and Downey's apothecary shop.

49. General store of Benjamin D. Wilson.

50. Maximo Alaniz' townhouse.

51. John Goller's wagon-shop.

52. Juan Lanfranco's home and business office. (Site of later Lanfranco Building built by Juan and Mateo Lanfranco.)

53. Manuel Requena's home.

54. Bell Row—later Mellus Row—owned first by Captain Alexander Bell, later by Henry Mellus. Fremont's headquarters in 1847.

55. José del Carmen Lugo's townhouse.

56. José Vicente Guerrero's home.

57. Juan Apablasa's home.

58. Fort Moore. (What is left of Fort Moore Hill is today occupied by administrative offices of Los Angeles City Board of Education, just east of which is the Pioneer Memorial.)

59. Benjamin S. Eaton's home.

60. Zanja Madre (mother canal), by which early settlers and later townsmen got water from the Los Angeles River for irrigation and drinking.

61. United States Hotel.

II

A Spanish Pueblo is Founded

FROM SIMPLE BEGINNINGS as a tule-hut Pueblo on the Porciúncula River has come the fabulous city of Los Angeles.

The story of the first settlers of this Pueblo, who were willing to leave established homes in Mexico and make a heartbreaking journey through frontier country for the purpose of starting a new community in an unknown land, is one of courage and persistence. The people who gave up old Mexico for new California were *paisanos*, true countrymen, the best who could be recruited for the purpose, men and women who could stand heat and hardship and who knew how to work in the fields.

On September 4, 1781, they had completed the last lap of their long journey. Sometime during the morning of that day, probably after an early mass, they left San Gabriel to begin the four-league trip that would take them to their planned destination. Men, women, and children, riding mules or horses, with mules to carry their belongings, made up the party. They were escorted by four young soldiers, assigned at San Gabriel, headed by Corporal José Vicente Feliz, a veteran of Anza's second overland expedition to California from Sonora. The colonists left San Gabriel eagerly, for they had been quarantined there seventeen days.

Stirring up clouds of dust, they followed the Indian trail that today is Mission Road, crossed the area now within Alhambra's boundaries, touched the southern border of present-day Lincoln Park, and arrived at the east bank of the wide bed of the Los Angeles River. The trail led them across a sandy waste, through green willows and tule growth. It took them by a giant sycamore that was a landmark then and in later years. The colonists splashed through the rippling stream, which was shallow enough to ford. The trail they followed became Aliso Street, named for the huge sycamore which was called "El Aliso." It led to the river bank at its lowest point. They climbed the black and loamy soil. Almost at once they reached the level area, well covered with grass, that had been chosen for plaza, house lots, and planting fields. In this higher area were occasional groups of cottonwood trees which sent drifts of fluffy seed into the air. Here and there were sycamores with richly-colored leaves and irregular branching habits.

To the west or rear of the pueblo site, and not far away, were low, rounding hills, covered sparsely with grass that had turned brown and a scattering of chaparral and cactus clumps. To the immediate north were other brown hills through which the river entered the valley from unseen sources. Farther to the north were the high, blue San Gabriel Mountains.

The packtrain party was not unobserved as it crossed the river and climbed the bank. Indians from Yang-na, the adjacent village, had been watching the newcomers. These short, stocky Indians, Shoshonean in speech, were curious and friendly. They came from their clusters of brush huts set among cottonwoods and sycamores somewhat to the south, near the river bank and

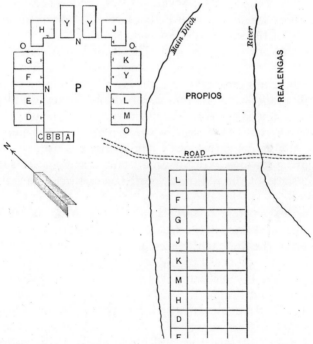

The plan of the Pueblo of Los Angeles in 1786, showing 50-foot house lots at the upper left around the Plaza and 7-acre farm lots, [out of proportion to the house lots] at lower right. The main ditch and the Los Angeles River are shown, and between them the rental lands. Across the river are the commons and pasture lands.

(From Bancroft)

[11]

high enough to be safe from the river's vagaries during annual rainy seasons. Yang-na men and women pressed forward to observe their new neighbors. If they were keeping to original native ways, the men wore no clothes, and the women wore deerskin skirts and heavy necklaces. If San Gabriel had made its impress, as seems likely, they wore the simple and basic garb of neophytes.

The Yang-na folk were familiar with Spanish-speaking people, for since 1771, when Mission San Gabriel was founded, they had helped wear smooth the trail from their village to the establishment of the Franciscan missionary priests. Still earlier, in 1769, they had greeted the first white visitors to their region: the members of the pioneering Portolá party, who were following a coastal route north from San Diego, with the Bay of Monterey as the objective. Under the command of Gaspar de Portolá of the Spanish Army, this first land expedition, a procession of scouts, leaders, priests, retainers, and a huge packtrain, passed through the Los Angeles area early in August. The story is preserved in several diaries, the most readable and detailed of which is that of Father Crespi, who wrote enthusiastically of the site of Los Angeles.

Of the very spot where the Pueblo of Los Angeles was to arise twelve years later, Crespi commented that it had "all the requisites for a large settlement." He noted "a large vineyard of wild grapes" and "an infinity of rose bushes in full bloom." He pronounced the soil "capable of producing every kind of grain and fruit." He recorded that a number of villagers who "live in this delightful place among the trees on the river" brought gifts of baskets of pinole and strings of shell beads, while some of the old men "puffed at us three mouthfuls of smoke."

The best current research indicates that Yang-na—or Yabit, as the name appears in the records of Mission San Gabriel—was located in the area of the present City Hall and probably on the site of the pioneer Los Angeles hotel, the Bella Union.

It was the Portolá party which had given the Los Angeles River its mouth-filling name: Nuestra Señora la Reina de Los Angeles de Porciúncula, which means "Our Lady, Queen of the Angels of Porciúncula." This was on August 2, 1769. The day before had been the jubilee day of the Lady, hence the name.[1] The river's name was shortened to Porciúncula.

---

[1] It was in the church dedicated to the Lady, in the village of Porciúncula, Italy, that St. Francis, founder of the Franciscan order, is said to have gained his jubilee or year of remission from the penal consequence of sin.

The Indian village of Yang-na occupied a site adjacent to that later chosen for the Pueblo of Los Angeles. The villagers were Shoshonean in speech. *Sketch by Cal N. Peters to illustrate Arthur Woodward's "Indian Foodstuffs of Los Angeles County," Courtesy of Los Angeles Museum, History Division.*

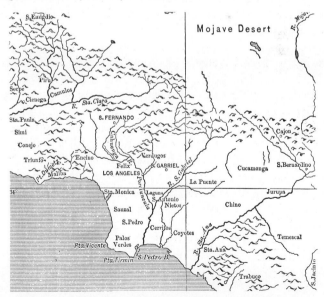

The Los Angeles District, 1800-1830. *(From Bancroft)*

The Pueblo which arose on the west bank of the Porciúncula became logically El Pueblo de Nuestra Señora la Reina de Los Angeles de Porciúncula. This was usually shortened to "El Pueblo" in both Spanish and Mexican periods and, in the American, to "Los Angeles" or even, alas, to "Los" or "L. A."

The founding on September 4, 1781—even among a ceremony-loving people—did not consist of processions, speeches, fanfare, or music. Mostly it consisted of tired, dusty, and sweaty people unpacking their mules and getting temporarily settled. For the men this meant making shelters of branches and tule. For the women it meant segregating and washing clothes and bringing water for cooking and drinking. For the children it may have meant splashing in the river.

Doubtless Corporal Feliz had first pointed out to each of the eleven heads of families the location of his particular house lot and planting field, areas already assigned in a drawing that had taken place at San Gabriel.

The founding of the Pueblo of Los Angeles followed closely the pattern of the founding, four years earlier, of the Pueblo of San José on the Guadalupe River southeast of San Francisco Bay. Both foundings had been well planned and were accomplished under the direct orders of Governor Felipe de Neve. In the case of San José, an army lieutenant escorted the settlers down from the Presidio of San Francisco. For Los Angeles, an army corporal performed the same function. Both foundings were civil affairs which did not call for the presence of governor, officials, or priests. Both pueblos started as tule-hut farming communities.

Unfortunately there seems to have been no diary kept of the founding of Los Angeles. Corporal Feliz, the "little father of the Pueblo" and its guiding spirit during the early years, and Private Roque de Cota were perhaps the only ones present who had that rare accomplishment, the ability to write. The corporal's name survives in Rancho Los Feliz (of which he became the owner) and in Los Feliz Boulevard, a well-known Los Angeles thoroughfare. If details of the founding are uncertain and unavailable, much is known of the settlers themselves for the program of recruiting and supplying these people, even to item-by-item records of clothes and equipment, has been preserved.[2]

As the forty-four "pobladores" sat about their camps that first evening their minds were full of the memories of the hard journey that had begun seven months before, on the morning of February 2, in Los Álamos, Sonora. There had been vast excitement in that mining town, for assembled there—ready for the start—were the settlers who had been signed up in various Sonora and Sinaloa villages by Captain Fernando Javier Rivera y Moncada. Men, women, and children—all dressed and outfitted for the trip and for frontier settlement—were milling about. Saddle and pack mules were kicking up a lot of dust. And with the party, ready for the go signal, was the escort of seventeen soldier recruits, gaily garbed in new blue jackets bright with epaulettes and yellow buttons. The wives and children of the soldiers were with them, too, for they also were going to California.

The memories of that day and of succeeding days were vivid. Under military command, the cavalcade of colonists and soldiers took the road that led to the mouth of the Mayo River, and launches got them across the wide Gulf of California to Loreto in Lower California. Another sea voyage brought them to San Luis Gonzaga Bay. They rested at Mission Santa María, then started on the terrific overland trip to San Diego. They had been exposed to smallpox and two of their number were left behind. On reaching San Diego they could forget forbidding deserts, grim mountains, and dangers. Some of the soldiers remained at the Presidio. The rest of the party arrived at San Gabriel August 18. Because of the smallpox scare they were quarantined a league from the Mission. A few days later, on August 26, Governor Neve drafted his detailed instructions for the founding of Los Angeles, the laying out of its plaza and building lots, together with the distribution of the lots and the planting lands "in the name of the King—equally and proportionately to all settlers"—together with provision for the erection "at the proper time" of a church, governmental buildings, and other offices. Even before the settlers arrived at San Gabriel the governor probably had founding plans well worked out, for he had been at the Mission since early May.

Now that the journey was over, the final trip from San Gabriel to the Porciúncula River must have seemed easy. And as they unpacked, the sight of certain belongings must have brought back pleasant memories of visiting the well-stocked shelves of their hometown shops and of picking out—with the approval of Captain Rivera—everything from shoes to hair

---

[2]The best summaries and translations of original documents relating to the founding of Los Angeles are contained in the 1931 *Annual Publication* of the Historical Society of Southern California, which commemorated the 150th anniversary of the founding. To Thomas Workman Temple II goes major credit for the work of translation and for exhaustive historical and genealogical research upon the subject of the founders and of the soldiers who accompanied them from Mexico.

First white men to visit the Los Angeles area were members of the Portolá party in 1769. The soldiers were called "leather-jackets." *Sketch by Cal N. Peters to illustrate Arthur Woodward's "California Leather Jackets of 1769," Courtesy of Los Angeles County Museum, History Division.*

ribbons. Rivera not only had supplied them amply, but had offered each recruit ten pesos a month and daily rations from enlistment, as well as promising stock, tools, utensils, and a five-year moratorium on taxes in the new pueblo.

If there were any campfires that first night, one of them must have revealed the strong, young face of Antonio Villavicencio, the first recruit, a native of Chihuahua, who had enlisted at Villa Sinaloa on May 30, 1780. Antonio's wife, María, was with him, as was their eight-year-old adopted daughter, María. (Almost all the first women of Los Angeles were named María.)

The oldest man in the crowd was 67-year-old Basilio Rosas from Durango, while the youngest of the heads of families was Alejandro Rosas of Rosario. Alejandro's wife was Juana, whom he married after enlisting. The 25 pesos it cost them to get married was the first item in the expense account kept for the young husband.

There were other settlers present that evening, and their musical names roll out of the old records—José de Lara, José Vanegas (who would be named the first *alcalde* or mayor), Pablo Rodríguez, José Antonio Navarro, Luis Quintero, Manuel Camero, José Moreno, Antonio Mesa, and their families.

In addition there were the four young men in soldier uniform. Corporal Feliz, already mentioned, would guide and govern the little pueblo in its first years. His wife had died during the first night of the Anza expedition while giving birth to a "fine boy." With Feliz now were Roque Jacinto de Cota, his brother Antonio de Cota, and Francisco Salvador Lugo. The last named was the father of a six-year-old boy, Antonio María Lugo, who was destined to become a famous land and cattle owner, to symbolize the California *ranchero*, and to be one of Los Angeles' most important citizens.

Such were the people—men of the soil—who founded the city of Los Angeles a month and a half before the British surrendered to Washington at Yorktown, nearly ten years before the site of the capital city of the United States was selected, and twenty-four years before the Lewis and Clark expedition crossed the continent. In a few years or a few decades the eleven families would be swallowed up in the stream of California life. The children married other Californians or Indians of nearby villages, including Yang-na, and today there are very few people who can trace their kinship to the pioneer founders. They did their jobs, but the soldiers and later immigrants became the *rancheros* and political leaders whose names and activities were known through the Spanish and Mexican periods.

The founding of Los Angeles was part of Spanish plans for the colonization of Upper California through the establishment there of missions, presidios, and pueblos. These plans developed as a part of the expansionist program of José de Gálvez, adviser to King Charles III, working through the obliging viceroy of New Spain. Soldiers led the way and, carrying out royal orders, built and maintained along the coast the presidios of San Diego, Monterey, San Francisco, and Santa Barbara. These frontier outposts permitted the building and insured the protection of missions and pueblos in the interior. Governor Neve, traveling north from Loreto, in Lower California, to Monterey, in Upper California, several years before 1781, had selected the pueblo sites of Los Angeles and San José. Detailed regulations —the *Reglamento*—issued over Neve's signature in 1779 and receiving royal approval in 1781, covered the setting up and maintenance of the Pueblo of Los Angeles, with generous provision for the welfare of the settlers.

The first census of Los Angeles, dated at San Gabriel November 19, 1781, showed the settlers had earthen-roofed huts (made of willow branches interlaced with tule). These were ready none too soon, for already dry winds from the north were alternating with hints of winter rains. These rains, the settlers would soon learn, could change a mild rippling stream into a purple turmoil. The census also showed that each head of a family had two fields for the planting of corn, together with a plowshare, a hoe, and an axe. In addition to the cattle, horses, and mules distributed to the settlers, the community had a number of carts, wagons, and breeding animals. Probably by this time a dam had been built at a place on the river above the town, as well as the main canal—the *zanja-madre*—to divert water for irrigation. Next to shelter, the construction of dam and canal were first aims of the Pueblo. The canal extended southwesterly between village and planting fields. From the village, on higher ground, the townsmen had a full view of farming operations, all of which were carried on in the river-rich area southeast of present day Main Street. The community-owned fields lay to the northeast of the road (later Aliso Street) by which the party had come from San Gabriel. The privately assigned fields were to the southwest, extending perhaps as far as today's East Fourth Street.

A distinguished visitor rode into the Pueblo the evening of March 18, 1782. He was a grey-robed priest, Junípero Serra, founder and president of the missions of California. Probably he was the first overnight guest. In the morning he hurried on to San Gabriel.

Don Vicente Lugo's town house facing the Plaza. In the rear vineyards and planted fields. Photo 1857. *Courtesy Title Insurance and Trust Company.*

Three days later three heads of families—Lara, Mesa, and Quintero—were expelled from the Pueblo, forfeiting their lands and stock. Did this action follow a recommendation of Father Serra, or was Corporal Feliz merely on the job and doing an unpleasant duty?

By 1784 Los Angeles began to look like a village of old Mexico, for the makeshift huts had given way to adobe houses and a chapel had been built. Except when a priest visited them, however, pious Angelenos still had to travel four leagues to hear mass. Possibly by that time townsmen had begun using, as roofing material, tar from the pits now called "La Brea," located eight miles west on the Indian trail to the beach. In the fall of that year several retirement-minded soldiers at the Presidio of San Diego got permission from the governor—then Pedro Fages—to put cattle on lands of their own choosing outside the four square leagues of land of the Pueblo of Los Angeles. This was the beginning of the rancho period, so important to the development of Los Angeles as trading and social center for the ranchos that ultimately ringed the Pueblo.

On Los Angeles' fifth birthday, September 4, 1786, an important ceremony took place. Governor Fages commissioned one of his army men at the Presidio of Santa Barbara—which had jurisdiction over the Los Angeles area—to put the settlers officially in possession. José Argüello, in charge of the Santa Barbara Company, had this assignment. He came to Los Angeles and appointed Corporal Feliz and Private Roque de Cota to act as legal witnesses. Only eight of the original heads of families were left, but a new head and his family had joined the colony, Francisco Sinavo. All stood in the hot sun of the Plaza, as one by one the men were called to step forward. Antonio Villavicencio was the first to be summoned as he was the first to enlist. To him was officially granted his house lot, his farm lots, and finally a registered branding iron by which his cattle could be distinguished from those of his neighbors. Argüello explained to him his rights and obligations, which included, of course, the paying of taxes henceforth, and Villavicencio replied that he understood fully. After him each of the other heads was given a grant and a branding iron. Each recipient signed the papers with a cross. Surely the best San Gabriel wine was used that evening to toast the sovereign, the commissioner from Santa Barbara, the witnesses, the grantees, and the Pueblo.

Presently Corporal Feliz, of whom the settlers rarely complained, was given a promotion. He was made a *comisionado*, in effect a city manager, for he managed the Pueblo, its *alcalde*, and the other officials. He was responsible to the governor, through the Santa Barbara *comandante*, and he had to see that the settlers performed their duties and enjoyed their privileges. He helped the *alcalde* maintain order, justice, and morality. He carried out the rules laid down for dealing with and hiring Indians of the area as laborers.

By the end of the decade Felipe de Neve's hope had become a reality. The Pueblo's population was 139, including men who would play important parts in Southern California's story. Heads of families numbered 28. There were 29 dwellings, all of adobe, a town hall, a chapel, barracks, guardhouse, and granaries—these structures surrounded by an adobe wall like that of a medieval town. Outside were a few buildings. Los Angeles could boast, and did boast, that it produced more grain than any of the missions except that of neighboring San Gabriel. Congratulations were in order and Governor Fages was felicitated by the *Comandante General* for the progress made.

Don Antonio María Lugo, Ranchero and Pueblo leader, as portrayed by Henri Penelon. *Courtesy of History Division, Los Angeles County Museum.*

Don Vicente Lugo, "Beau Brummel" of El Pueblo, whose town-house faced the Plaza. From a painting. *Courtesy Title Insurance and Trust Company.*

The bull-and-bear fight was a favorite sport in El Pueblo.

III

Rancho Days

 EARLY IN RANCHO DAYS the Pueblo of Los Angeles began to develop into Southern California's trading, shopping, and social center. It had started as a farming community in 1781. Presently it became the heart of the cow country, for the ranchos that gradually encircled it and that finally extended from the seacoast to the foothills of the San Gabriel Mountains were devoted to the raising of long-horned cattle. By the middle of the 1840s rancho days were at their height and nowhere in California did the pastoral period see a greater flowering than in and around the little Mexican town of Los Angeles.

The Pueblo had grown up about its Plaza—not the original Plaza of the first settlers, but one that almost adjoined it on the southeast. The original Plaza had been discarded when the town began to expand. A church was needed and this called for a new and uncluttered public square. Started in 1818 on community-owned lands and finished in the early 1820s, the church dominated this new Plaza—just as it still does—and around the other sides of the Plaza arose the town houses of the *rancheros*.

From this center several dusty lanes extended, like the spokes of a lopsided wheel. They led northerly, easterly, southerly, and westerly through the one-story, flat-roofed town, through vineyards, cornfields, and grassy plains and valleys. Following the lines of least resistance they reached or passed the forty or more large ranchos in the present Los Angeles County area. One road led, of course, to Mission San Gabriel, the same road or pathway that the first settlers had taken when coming to found the Pueblo. Another, the development of an old Indian trail, reached the tar pits, eight miles west, where brea was available for roofs. *Calle Principal*, or Main Street, ultimately found its way through the Puerto Suelo into the San Fernando Valley and to Mission San Fernando. Eternity Street, now

North Broadway, led to the cemetery *(Campo Santo)*, started when it no longer was practical to bury in the lots immediately adjoining the church. One road led to San Pedro Bay, where cattle hides could be traded for the useful or fascinating imports of sea captains, another to the Redondo region, where salt could be obtained. There were roads leading across the

Plaza, about 1869. Rear of Church in foreground, Lugo House in background. On the left, buried in trees, the Jones-Simpson adobe; together with the Olvera House. *Photo by Vischer. Courtesy of Title Insurance and Trust Company.*

Santa Ana River to the ranchos of the San Diego area, while others meandered into the favored Santa Barbara region, almost solidly rancho country. The life of the inland Pueblo was supplemented by the lively presidio towns of San Diego and Santa Barbara on the coast.

If these roads led out to the ranchos, they also led into the Pueblo. Over them galloped the *rancheros* who came into Los Angeles to arrange cattle deals, to see what was new in saddles, to visit the liquor shops, play a little *monte* in a gambling house, or perhaps see a horse race or a bullfight, or even a bear-and-bullfight. Usually they called on friends, and occasionally on the priest—especially if a baptism, a wedding, or a burial was being arranged. The women of the ranchos, with town houses in which to stop, looked for bargains in furniture and hard-

[23]

ware from New England, shawls from China, or *rebozos, serapes*, and pointed shoes from San Blas, Mazatlán, and Acapulco. They went to parties and balls. When a Pueblo shopkeeper heard a creaking of *carreta* wheels and the barking of packs of town dogs he knew that a party of women dressed in their best was arriving from one of the outlying ranchos.

Other members of a rancho's feudal organization also came into the Pueblo for business or fun. One large rancho might support several hundred persons: the owner, his big family, the poor relations, those people of special skills who helped make his place self-sustaining—the harness makers, wool-combers, tanners, and carpenters—the *majordomo* or superintendent, and a retinue of Indian vaqueros and servants. All found El Pueblo entrancing, whether they came to visit a shop or the church, attend a fandango or a party in a town house. When night settled down over the adobe village, however, only the glare from a building where a dance was in progress or from the lantern in front of a wineshop or tavern prevented heavy blackness from swallowing Los Angeles.

When Southern California cattle were in greatest demand—in the early 1850s, because of the Gold Rush—the ranchos round about the Pueblo presented "a lively spectacle," according to spectator Horace Bell. "The vast herds of cattle," he wrote, "and their number seemed absolutely without limit, the many picturesque horsemen driving the neighing and snorting herds in all directions, the retainers of the Lugos, the Dominguez, Ávilas and Sepúlvedas, the Stearns and Temples, all of whose herds ranged over the plains referred to, made quite an army, and from early dawn to the shades of evening were continually on the move, with jingling spurs, cavorting steeds and whizzing riatas." Next to the *alcaldes*, the "judges of the plains" —in charge of rodeos—were the most important officials of rancho days.

The growth from the walled Pueblo of the first decade to the southland's shopping, business, and social center had been gradual. It coincided with the rise of ranchos and their development. The impact of ranchos and rancho living on El Pueblo began three years after the founding. In the fall of 1784 three soldiers of the Presidio of San Diego bearing the now well-known names of Dominguez, Verdugo, and Nieto and thinking about retirement, got permission to place horses and cattle in areas near Los Angeles. Permission came from Don Pedro Fages, who was military commander and governor. Acting under the provisions of the Laws of the Indies, which governed New Spain, he said *yes* to the soldiers' requests but cautioned the applicants to do no injury to the Mission of San Gabriel, the Pueblo of Los Angeles, or the villages of Indians. The governor's authority was limited to lands outside the four-square-league area of El Pueblo, the exact boundaries of which no one then knew.

The three Spanish soldiers, apparently acting together, had petitioned for land on which to place their stock—presumably obtained from the surplusage of cattle and horses at the Presidio or at Mission San Diego.

Sixty-five-year-old Juan José Dominguez, who had been a soldier-member—a "leather-jacket"—of the pioneering Portolá party of 1769, led the way north from San Diego. He drove before him a herd of horses and two hundred head of cattle to the site he had picked on land facing San Pedro Bay. He built a house and several huts and corrals on the slope of a hill overlooking the river. The river was the San Gabriel, for many years would pass before the San Gabriel and the Los Angeles rivers traded channels. Dominguez was California's first *ranchero* and, under the elastic provisions of the concessions or "grants" of Spanish days, he became the acknowledged owner of Rancho San Pedro, the vague boundaries of which originally included at least 75,000 acres. During the two decades he lived on this rancho his cattle increased in number, grazing upon the rolling land that stretched to the mud flats that became Wilmington and upon the hills rising back of San Pedro Bay. Often Dominguez went into the Pueblo on business, to be transacted there in the "Officers' House."

The second of the presidio's soldiers obtained a concession to place cattle and horses on a great triangular area, the southern tip of which touched the Pueblo on the north. This man was Corporal José María Verdugo, the youngest of the three soldiers who had asked Fages for ranchos. Verdugo had picked the site while on "detached" service at the Mission of San Gabriel. It was close by, and in his mind's eye he saw his own cattle pastured there, his own water dam—like the one of the Pueblo's first settlers—and his own irrigated fields. He was not yet ready for retirement, so sent his brother Mariano ahead to get the place ready for him. Mariano built a house, planted a garden and vineyard, and looked after the stock on what became known as Rancho San Rafael, 36,000-acre site of present-day Glendale and part of Burbank. As the years rolled by the rancho supported "the retired corporal with the grade of sergeant," his children and his grandchildren, their crops, and their large herds of cattle and horses. Many hides from San Rafael went to San Pedro and thence by ship to New York and Boston. Verdugo fiestas and rodeos are remembered to this day.

The third pioneering *ranchero* was Manuel Nieto who, after leaving San Diego, settled first in the San Gabriel Valley—too close to the Mission for the liking of the priests—and ultimately in the fertile region southwest of the present city of Whittier. By the year 1800 his cattle were grazing the immense grass-covered plain that stretched as far south as the bluffs overlooking the Pacific Ocean. On the northwest his cattle wandered to the San Gabriel River and sometimes mixed with the stock of Dominguez, who owned the land across the river. Nieto's longhorns ranged southeast, through deep grass, to the Santa Ana River. The northerly limit of this 167,000-acre rancho was Camino Viejo, the old road that led from the Pueblo to San Diego. With Nieto's permission, farmers settled in the area near his home. The produce of their cornfields and vineyards helped supply the wants of the growing Pueblo. When divided among Nieto's heirs in the Mexican period, the sprawling Spanish rancho was re-granted by the Mexican Government as five ranchos: Santa Gertrudes, Los Coyotes, Los Alamitos, Los Cerritos, and Las Bolsas.

The "little father of the Pueblo," José Vicente Feliz, was rewarded with a rancho, possibly as early as the year 1795. Rancho Los Feliz adjoins the Pueblo on the northwest and is today within Los Angeles city limits—one large portion of it being Griffith Park.

The Wolfskill home located in El Pueblo in Southern California's first commercial orange grove, later to become the site of the Southern Pacific Depot. Photo, 1880s; *Courtesy Title Insurance and Trust Company.*

Seven additional ranchos were granted in the Los Angeles area before the end of the Spanish regime in California in 1822. Most ranchos of the region, however, were Mexican in origin. With the missions finally secularized, 1834-1836, after long pressure on the Government from political leaders and the increasing white population, a land rush—literally—took place. The missions themselves were turned into parish churches, with secular clergy substituted for missionary priests. The greater number of the local Indians, demoralized and helpless, flocked into the Pueblo to create unhappy problems for *alcaldes*, councilmen, and townsmen. Most of the vast holdings in land of Mission San Gabriel and Mission San Fernando were open to private claim—as were those of the other missions—and passed quickly into the hands of favored individuals who had the ear of the governor. As in Spanish days, ranchos were the gift of the Government. By the middle 1840s most of the Los Angeles County area lying west of the San Gabriel Mountains and outside the boundaries of the Pueblo was covered by a pattern of ranchos owned by soldiers, ex-soldiers, officials, leaders, and a few naturalized citizens of European and American origin.

The activities of these *rancheros*, together with those of their families and dependents, revolved about and centered in El Pueblo. Moreover, these people were proud of El Pueblo de Los Angeles, for in 1845 the town was made in fact the capital of Alta California. Governor Pío Pico established his headquarters in a one-story adobe building on *Calle Principal*, the former store of *ranchero*-merchant Isaac Williams, which later would be transformed into the Bella Union Hotel, "the finest hotel south of San Francisco!" Actually, Los Angeles had been decreed to be the capital in 1835, but the Monterey officials—comfortable in their charming setting—had resisted the move south for a whole decade. Aware of the honor that had come finally to the city, the Los Angeles *ayuntamiento* or council declared on April 19, 1845, for the repair and white-washing of the town's buildings. "Although it is a small city," agreed the councilmen, "it should proceed to show its cleanliness, magnificence and brilliance in such a manner that the traveler who visits us may say, 'I have seen the City of the Angels. I have seen its police and all demonstrated that it is the Mexican paradise.'" Paradise or not, the Plaza of El Pueblo continued to be the center of community life for townsmen and for visitors from outlying ranchos.

This Plaza was in the making when the site for the church was chosen in 1818 by Governor Solá. The site was not the

The Vaquero, as painted by James Walker (1818-1889). *Courtesy Mrs. Reginald Walker of Oakland.*

first. The one selected four years earlier and facing the original Plaza was abandoned in favor of this better location near the house of the *comisionado*. Townsmen—and there were about six hundred of them—subscribed five hundred cattle to the building fund, supplemented a year later by seven barrels of brandy, valued at $575, contributed by Mission San Gabriel. The sale of cattle and brandy to pious Angelenos brought in cash—and before 1821 the walls were up to the window arches. So far, though, Los Angeles had obtained no chaplain, even though an appeal had been made to the viceroy himself on behalf of Army veterans who were spending their declining years in Los Angeles without spiritual care. The priests at San Gabriel felt that they could not take care of the Pueblo and the ranchos while meeting all the problems of their own mission and its far-flung outposts.

While the church was being built the Spanish regime in California yielded to the Mexican, as a result of successful revolt in Mexico. At Monterey, the capital city, allegiance to the new government was sworn on April 11, 1822. A legislative assembly was established. The *ayuntamiento* or council form of city government was fully established in Los Angeles in November.

The church was so nearly finished on December 8, 1822, that it could be formally dedicated. Work had stopped in the fall of 1821, when funds ran out—even though some citizens drank "immense quantities" of brandy "in their zeal for the spiritual welfare of the town," to quote historian Hubert Howe Bancroft. To take care of the emergency, Padre Payeras appealed to the various missions to contribute cattle, laborers, or anything for the completion of the church and a house for the priest. The missions responded: San Miguel with 500 cattle, San Luis Obispo with 200 cattle, and Santa Barbara with one barrel of brandy. San Diego sent two barrels of white wine, Purísima six mules and 200 cattle, San Fernando one barrel of brandy, and San Gabriel two barrels of brandy. From San Gabriel's *asistencia* at San Bernardino came handmade furniture. San Buenaventura offered to try to make up deficits or supply furniture. A heavy fine imposed on two eminent Angelenos caught smuggling at Malibu went to the church. Generous Don Francisco Ávila is said to have presented a brace of bells to call townsmen to devotions. Years later, in 1830, a 50-pound bell came from Captain Henry Fitch. The gift of this heavy bell was the penance imposed on Fitch for scandalizing — and delighting — *Californios* by his elopement with the charming daughter of Joaquin Carrillo, prominent San Diegan.

A tower of strength in the physical completion of the church was Joseph Chapman, the first American to settle in the Los Angeles area. This "regenerated pirate," to use Robert G. Cleland's phrase, had talents as a carpenter, blacksmith, jack-of-all-trades, and amateur surgeon which made him the most popular and useful man in Southern California. Claiming to have been shanghaied in the Sandwich Islands, Chapman was a member of the coast-raiding party of Hypolyte Bouchard, which sacked and burned Monterey in 1818. Chapman and two sailors went ashore from the *Santa Rosa* and were arrested. Chapman was taken to Southern California, where the missionary priests soon discovered that the prisoner knew how to build a grist mill, how to fell a tree, construct a schooner, splint broken bones, boss a gang of Indians, pull teeth, fashion farm implements, and make soap. When he arrived in San Gabriel in 1821 to build a grist mill similar to the one he had built at Mission Santa Inez, he became a favorite of Father Sánchez. The friar marveled that this strong young man, who had been so long "in the darkness of Baptist faith" could give such an example of true piety to older Christians. Chapman had practiced logging in the state of Maine and was given the job of obtaining needed lumber for the church at Los Angeles. With a band of Mission Indians, he established a lumber camp in a high mountain canyon above the present site of Pasadena. The logs he got were rolled down the canyon sides and hauled by oxen to the Plaza in Los Angeles, ultimately to help sustain the church.

Chapman exerted a civilizing influence on the Pueblo whose founders had been provided originally only with plowshares, hoes, and axes. For a long time the importation of tools, furniture, and clothing was either forbidden by law or was made difficult by excessive customs duties. Chapman was rewarded by being pardoned, naturalized, baptised into the Catholic Church, and allowed to marry the girl (Guadalupe Ortega) whose family's ranch home near Santa Barbara had been burned by his former companions during their devastating course down the coast. Blond Joe, as he was called, bought a home in Los Angeles, planted 4,000 grapevines from Mission cuttings, and continued to serve San Gabriel and the area. His descendants today are proud of their "pirate" ancestor.

Increasing trade with American vessels gradually lifted the standards of living in the Pueblo and on the ranchos. Californians and ship captains either evaded or defied the law, and

Don Abel Stearns, merchant and land owner, a naturalized Mexican citizen, settled in Los Angeles in 1833, became the wealthiest man in California, and married Arcadia Bandini. *Courtesy Title Insurance and Trust Company.*

smuggling came to be considered one of the necessary and civilizing activities of life—as indeed it was. Only the customs officers felt dishonored by its practice. The importation of tables, benches, stools, and beds made life more comfortable on ranchos and in town and caused shops to arise near the Plaza—following the completion of the church. Suits embroidered with gold and silver thread, *rebozos* of silk and cotton, calicoes, white muslin, and percale—all these began to find their way into the Pueblo. Rooms were added to existing homes. New homes were built with larger floor plans. Wants increased and wants were satisfied. With the arrival, in the 1830s and 1840s, of pack-train caravans from Santa Fé, New Mexico, bringing a great variety of manufactured goods to be traded for horses and mules, Californians could get about everything they needed or wanted.

Probably the first man to build a home directly facing the new Plaza was José Antonio Carrillo, influential politician—and owner of ranchos—who liked to name governors or dethrone them. A handsome man of iron constitution, it is said of him that no Californian could drink as much brandy as he and with so little effect. As the rising walls of the church began to dominate the Plaza area, Don José petitioned his brother Anastacio Carrillo, then the town's *comisionado*, for a house lot to face the Plaza at its southwest corner. He wanted one near the "new temple which is being built for the benefit of our Holy Religion." The petition was granted, and Don José began building on the site of the present Pico House. One wing extended along *Calle Principal,* now Main Street, and another ran back from its eastern terminus to a cross wall, thus enclosing a patio. The building had white walls and a high, gabled roof of red tiles—one of the few tiled roofs in town. In its ample ballroom "the beauty and the chivalry of the Pueblo" met in many a happy gathering. When Pío Pico, the brother-in-law of its owner, married María Ygnacia Alvarado in 1834, the marriage feast, the most sumptuous and prolonged on record, was celebrated in this house. Festivities lasted eight days and were attended by all Los Angeles—and nearly everyone of importance from San Diego north.[3]

Plaza fronts became the fashion for those who could afford them. In the 1830s and 1840s many distinguished families had town houses around the square or as close to it as possible.

Next to the Carrillo place arose an adobe home which became Pío Pico's when he was California's governor in 1845-46. This generous, game-loving man, fond of horse racing, pretty girls, heavy jewelry, and official decorations, owned princely ranchos and, in politics, was an ardent Southern partisan. He participated in the province's sectional strife which occasionally broke out into armed revolt. His Plaza home was within walking distance of gubernatorial headquarters on *Calle Principal.* For years after the Americans came this home and one adjoining on the east remained the property of the Pico brothers, Pío and Andrés, though both spent most of their time on their ranchos.

On the east side of the Plaza arose two town houses which became famous as the del Valle place and the Lugo place. Earlier pioneers had built them, members of the Figueroa,

---

[3]Leo Carrillo, well known modern *Californio,* is not only a grandnephew of Don José but is an active member of the State Park Commission and of the group concerned with the restoration and maintenance of the Plaza and its environs.

Don José Sepúlveda, owner of Rancho San Joaquin, whose town house was near Eternity and Virgin streets. Don José was famous for his fast horses, his hospitality, and his lavish dress. As owner of *Black Swan* he won over Pio Pico's *Sarco* in a horserace witnessed by all of Southern California in 1852. From a painting by Henri Penelon, done in 1856. *Courtesy Charles W. Bowers Memorial Museum, Santa Ana.*

ROPING OF THE BEAR, by James Walker. *From the collection of the California Historical Society.*

Cattle Drive, by James Walker. *From the collection of the California Historical Society.*

Doña Mariana Coronel demonstrates the grinding of corn on a metate. From a painting by Alexander F. Harmer. *Courtesy Los Angeles County Museum.*

Typical costumes of rancho women. From a contemporary lithograph by Carlos Nebel. *Courtesy Los Angeles County Museum.*

Ballesteros, and Navarro families. Both houses were originally one-story buildings. The addition of second stories came apparently early in the 1850s. The southeast corner structure was the town house of Don Ygnacio del Valle of Rancho San Francisco. He had been soldier and holder of governmental offices until he took over the management of the rancho upon the death of his father, Antonio del Valle, in 1841. Presently he came to spend most of his time in the Pueblo, and in his Plaza home he raised a family of five children. Don Ygnacio became the *alcalde* of Los Angeles and when county government was organized he was the first recorder. Dignified and courteous, his presence lent social prestige to the Plaza and within the thick-walled enclosure of his home were held most of the political meetings of the early American period.

Adjoining del Valle's place was the town house of Don Vicente Lugo, who was famous for his horsemanship, for his elegant wardrobe, and for his famous father, Antonio María Lugo. The Lugos owned Rancho San Antonio, a huge Spanish grant adjoining the Pueblo on the southeast, and had ranch houses as well as town houses. The town dwelling of Lugo the elder was half a mile from the Plaza on the road to San Pedro, for Don Antonio preferred the quiet atmosphere there to the traffic and excitement of the Plaza. Don Vicente, like his father, was a cattle owner on a grand scale.

One of the finest of the Pueblo's town houses stood on the north side of the Plaza. Originally the home of Don Tiburcio Tapia of Rancho Cucamonga—a successful merchant and three times *alcalde*— it became the residence of Agustin Olvera, for whom Olvera Street was named. The *corredor* faced the Plaza while the building extended back along the east side of the lane

From the Plaza looking north over Sonoratown, Los Angeles. Plaza Church at left. *Courtesy Title Insurance and Trust Company.*

that became Olvera Street. Court proceedings were often held in this house, for Olvera was a judge of the first instance, named to that position by Military Governor Riley. Earlier, Judge Olvera, who came from Mexico in 1834, had held various important governmental offices and then studied law, becoming Los Angeles' pioneer lawyer. With the organization of the American government and Los Angeles County, Olvera became the first "county judge." Townsman though he was, he, too, was the owner of ranchos.

The favorite gambling game of visiting *rancheros* was *monte*. To accommodate them a large adobe gambling house, devoted to the operation of "monte banks," was built on the Plaza's north side—across the street from the Tapia-Olvera place. Its proprietor was Pedro Seguro (or Segureau). Horace Bell seems to be describing this building as it appeared in 1852, when *rancheros* had more cash in hand than they did in 1844-45. "We betook ourselves to Aleck Gibson's gambling house on the plaza," he wrote, "where a well kept bar was in full blast, and some half dozen *monte banks* in successful operation, each table with its green baize cover being literally heaped with piles of $50 ingots, commonly called slugs. Betting was high. You would frequently see a *ranchero* with an immense pile of gold in front of him, quietly and unconcernedly smoking his *cigarrito* and betting twenty slugs on the turn, the losing of which produced no perceptible discomposure of his grave countenance." Today the site of the gambling house is occupied by the Bank of America's building.

To name all the Southern Californios who had town houses close to the Plaza would be to give a roster of those who made history in the Pueblo. Just south of the burial ground of the church was the home of Don Andrés Pico, Pío's brother—who acquired fame as leader of the lance-bearing Californian forces at the Battle of San Pascual, disastrous to Americans, and later as generous host on Rancho Ex-Mission de San Fernando. It had been the home of Doña Benancia Sotel de Dominguez (who bought it from Carlos Baric), and whose daughters married into ranch-owning families. Directly south of the Plaza were the homes of fiery Don Vicente Sánchez of Rancho Paso de la Tijera, whose name was given to Sanchez Street when it was opened; of Don Francisco Sepúlveda of Rancho San Vicente y Santa Monica; and of Don Francisco O'Campo, whose quadrangular front yard—the "Plazuela" or "O'Campo's Plaza"—was given over to a favorite Pueblo sport, cockfighting. South of O'Campo's home was the residence of Don Ygnacio Coronel, a man of education and culture. In this house, begin-

Through the belfry of the Plaza Church can be seen the Plaza.
Courtesy Title Insurance and Trust Company.

ning in 1838, Don Ygnacio conducted a school, aided by the
$15 a month he got from Pueblo authorities.

North of the Olvera adobe was—and is—the Ávila House, a
large one-story adobe structure built by Francisco Ávila, one
of the sons of Cornelio Ávila, who settled in the Pueblo in
1783. Francisco was *alcalde* in 1810 and built this home when
Plaza and church plans were in the making—possibly as early as
the date often ascribed to it, 1818. The Ávila place, originally
much larger than now, figured prominently in Pueblo history
and in recent years has served to symbolize Pueblo days and to
stimulate the restoration of Olvera Street and the whole Plaza
area.

Among other worthies of Pueblo days whose names or town
houses were within easy walking (or fast galloping) distance
of the Plaza were members of the families of Alaniz, de Celis,
Sepúlveda, Lanfranco, Stearns, Temple, Keller, Coronel, Rocha, Lugo, Garfias, Aguilar, Ramírez, Requena, López, Val-
dez, Gallardo, Apablasa, Bell, Wilson, Mascarel, Macy, Manso,

[35]

Ranch home of Don Vicente Lugo on Rancho San Antonio which adjoined the Pueblo on the southeast. Photo taken in 1892. *Courtesy Title Insurance and Trust Company.*

Figueroa, Mellus, Ybarra, Bauchet, Ballesteros, Novarro, Vignes, Uribe, Sainsevain, Pryor and Chavez—musical names out of Los Angeles' past.[4]

The last mentioned name belonged to Julian Chavez, a young New Mexican who got to his miniature rancho from the Plaza by taking Eternity Street and turning west before reaching the *Campo Santo.* His home and his corrals later became Chavez Ravine, now the site of the major league baseball park of the Los Angeles Dodgers.

The center of interest of the people of the Pueblo and of the surrounding ranchos was the Plaza—"a treeless common; its surface pawed into ridges or trodden into dust by the hoofs of the numerous mustangs tethered on it or ridden over it."[5] It was the scene of tragedies, comedies, sports events, and religious processions. It echoed to the tread of armed men. It was the setting for fiestas and civic parades. Trappers, beginning with the Jedediah Smith party of 1826-27, mountain men and traders from New Mexico, Colorado, and Utah, often garbed like Indians, poured into the area for business and fun. So did Sonoran miners on their way to Placerita Canyon, north of

---

[4]The location of many of the town houses of the old Pueblo is shown on the map herein.

[5]J. M. Guinn, "The Story of a Plaza," in *Annual Publication* of the Historical Society of Southern California, 1899.

Mission San Fernando, where gold was discovered on March 9, 1842. Many a just-married couple came out the doors of the church to ride away on horseback with a retinue of friends. The Plaza was always the scene of men galloping in and out, raising clouds of yellow dust, and there was always the commotion caused by groups of saddled horses and ox-drawn carretas held by Indians who were awaiting owners seeing friends or in shops.

In its earliest period those who kept close watch on the Plaza might have witnessed there the punishment of offenders against morality and good order. Two women, it is recorded, were forced to expose themselves with shaved heads at the church door—"for scandalous conduct." To enter the church disrespectfully, to lounge at its door, to ride at unnecessary speed or at unusual hours—these acts subjected the guilty ones to arrest, fine, and punishment, perhaps at the public whipping post. Pueblo authorities made continuing efforts to exterminate idleness, vagrancy, swindling, prostitution, and blasphemy.

On Sundays, in early days, the Plaza was fenced in for bullfights. After services in the church, throngs poured out to watch them either from a town house veranda or from any spot where they could be safe from the bull's sharp horns. Rarely was a bull killed in the Plaza. When he was killed, it was done with a knife attached to a yard-long stick. The fun for the men was to chase the plunging animal on horseback, after he was tired out by the teasing of the cape-wavers, who also rode. They tried to upset the bull by grabbing and twisting his tail. After a tumble he was free to run the plains. Later a bull ring was built northwest of the Plaza on *Calle del Toro* (now Castelar Street)—its site that of the present day French Hospital. Henceforth gaming on the Plaza was limited to cockfighting in the Plazuela and *monte* in the large gambling house.

In the explosive and partly comic-opera contests between the partisans of the south and those of northern California, the Plaza played a supporting role. One morning the aristocrats of the Plaza fronts looked out their doors to see Captain Espinoza with his northern detachment camped in the public square. The northerners had stolen in during night hours after defeating the southerners at the battle of San Buenaventura. Espinoza's men proceeded to go from house to house to arrest leaders of the southern movement, including José Antonio Carrillo, Pío Pico, Andrés Pico, and the *alcalde* himself, Gil Ybarra. These men were marched north as prisoners. This happened in the civil war of 1837-38. In 1845 Pío Pico and General Castro mobilized forces in the Plaza to go forth—400 strong— to exchange cannon shots with Micheltorena's army. There were Americans in both armies and they preferred fraternizing to fighting. Casualties at this battle of Cahuenga were one horse killed and one mule wounded. The day after Micheltorena raised the white flag, Pío Pico became governor of California.

The Plaza was the setting for two important inauguration ceremonies. The first concerned Don Carlos Carrillo—sometimes called "the Pretender." On December 6, 1837, accompanied by a cavalcade, he crossed the Plaza, took the oath of office, and in the church listened to a solemn mass. Plaza fronts were illuminated for three nights and a big cannon boomed forth the tidings that Los Angeles was the capital. When the actual governor, Alvarado, came down from Monterey, however, the Pretender fled to San Diego. On New Year's Eve of 1842 Manuel Micheltorena, who had arrived from Mexico in August with a nondescript army, the nucleus of which was made up of ex-convicts, took the oath of office as governor in the two-story Sánchez building south of the Plaza. This was followed by an inauguration ball that lasted a week. Plaza fronts were again brilliant and the cannon boomed. Until the battle of Cahuenga, Micheltorena remained governor.

The same Sánchez building served for the banquet and grand ball given in January of 1843 in honor of Commodore Thomas ap Catesby Jones of the United States Navy, who had come down to Los Angeles to apologize for having raised the American flag over Monterey the preceding October on the false rumor that the United States had declared war on Mexico.

A town which tossed its rubbish into the streets, and where cattle were slaughtered in the house yards and the remains of carcasses thrown about for scavenger dogs and crows, could not be expected to keep its Plaza clean. And it did not. Real cleanups of Los Angeles' Plaza took place, however, on the occasion of fiestas and especially during a *Corpus Christi* festival. The imposing feature of the latter, held forty days after Easter, was the opening procession around the Plaza. At this time the Picos, the del Valles, the Lugos, the Olveras, and others built booths and erected altars in front of their homes. Starting from the church after the four o'clock service, the procession included girls dressed in white and carrying baskets of flowers, boys of the choir, and twelve men bearing candles and representing the apostles, together with the people of the Pueblo. The marchers proceeded slowly from altar to altar, pausing for worship at each. Having made the circuit of the

The venerable Don Pío Pico. *Courtesy Title Insurance and Trust Company.*

Plaza—and this might take two hours—the procession returned to the church for the conclusion of the services.

Christmas festivities at the Plaza sometimes included little dramas called *Los Pastores* (The Shepherds)—delightful survivals of medieval miracle plays—the actors in which were the Pueblo's best amateurs. Shepherds on their way to the Bethlehem manger, the Archangel Michael, a hermit, and the Devil himself were usually the characters of these plays, which provided plenty of fun and horseplay. The favorite personality, as portrayed, was the Devil, who had horns, tail, and cloven hooves. Musicians and singers participated. There were fireworks and the ringing of church bells. The final undoing of the Devil at the hands of St. Michael caused the Plaza to resound with shouts and merry laughter. The actors all had big appetites and never failed to visit the houses around the Plaza where they were treated to *buñuelos*, sweet cakes fried in grease.

Don Arturo Bandini, recalling the impressive mass that was held in the church at 4:00 o'clock on Christmas morning, attended by everyone not bedridden, wrote: "I remember the large number of beautiful and richly caparisoned horses that were tied to the railing surrounding the old plaza, the rays of the cold, rising Christmas sun reflected back from silver ornaments on headstall and saddle. So chilled from being tied out in the cold, the impatient and fiery creatures would welcome the appearance of their masters with loud neighs of welcome or stamping of hoofs. The elder gentlemen would go with slow and dignified steps to their more quiet steeds; but the younger men! Ah! here was the time and place for horsemanship, with the fair ones looking on so demurely, far more demure than their modern sisters. Still no glance or movement of grace escaped their sharp, bright eyes."[6]

While festivals were held in the Plaza for all to see, the houses around about and up and down *Calle Principal* and other streets were the settings the year round for the balls which were the passion of all *Californios*. A ball in celebration of a wedding lasted usually three days—and was frequently given in an arbor in front of the house. Participants ate, drank, and danced day and night. While some were resting and sleeping, others were dancing. Music was furnished by violinists, a guitarist, and singers. The *bamba*, the *zorrita*, the *sota*, the *contradanza*, the *jarabe*, the *fandango*, and the *jota*—these were the favorite dances.

For a number of decades rancho days, adobe days, pastoral living, dominated the Pueblo and its Plaza.

Then the American Army marched in.

---

[6]Don Arturo Bandini, *Navidad*, re-published in 1958 by the California Historical Society.

IV

Americans Take Over

THE PUEBLO OF LOS ANGELES appeared completely deserted to the sailors and marines of Commodore Robert F. Stockton and to the soldiers of Major John C. Frémont as they marched into town late in the afternoon of August 13, 1846. Bandsmen led the marchers, blaring forth "Hail Columbia" and "Yankee Doodle" to empty streets.

The men of Stockton and the men of Frémont had joined forces in the vineyards and cornfields just outside the heart of the Pueblo. Stockton's forces had come from San Pedro, Frémont's from San Diego. Their march on Los Angeles was part of the plan for a quick occupation of the ports and towns of California which had begun the month before at Monterey when the flag of the United States was raised by Commodore John D. Sloat on July 7. Included in the dusty procession were *carretas*, each drawn by four oxen, carrying guns, ammunition, and baggage. Some of the officers were mounted.

Frémont's troops stopped short of the Plaza and camped in a broad area where Aliso Street intersected the sprawling *Calle de los Angeles*. Stockton's sailors and marines took over Pío Pico's former headquarters on *Calle Principal*.

At sunset Commodore Stockton tried an experiment. He gave a band concert in the Plaza where not an Angeleno was in sight. His musicians were the first full band to come to California. Now, in Los Angeles, they gave their first concert.

As the concert began, wide-eyed children ventured down the hill which overlooked the Plaza. As the lively tunes continued, older people followed or came out of their darkened homes. Before the concert was over there was a circle of delighted *Californios* and their *vivas* were many.

The next day at sunset there was another hour of music. By this time people from the ranchos were in the circle of listeners, for they had heard of the wonderful performances. There was present, too, an old priest from Mission San Gabriel.

Deeply moved, he sat by the door of the church. He rose when introduced to the American officers and told them he had not heard a band since leaving Spain over fifty years before. "Ah! that music," he added, "will do more service to the conquest of California than a thousand bayonets."

Meanwhile, American guns had been planted on the hill commanding the town and proclamations had been issued signed by Stockton as "Commander-in-chief and governor of the Territory of California." The conquest appeared complete and there was no trace of Pío Pico or his military commander, General José Castro. Both of them actually had left the Pueblo several days earlier, heading for Mexico.

After two weeks in peaceful Los Angeles, Stockton decided that he and Frémont could safely withdraw. He left Archibald Gillespie in charge, with fifty men, and went to Monterey. A month passed. Then one evening a courier named Juan Flaco (Lean John) Brown galloped into Monterey, after a daredevil race from Los Angeles. He carried mysterious cigaret papers on which was written "Believe the bearer." When he learned that Stockton had gone to Yerba Buena (San Francisco), Brown pushed on and delivered the message to the Commodore aboard the *Congress*. Los Angeles is in revolt, he declared, and Gillespie is besieged on a hill by 600 Californians under the command of that arch foe of Americans, José María Flores.

It was true. Los Angeles and Southern California had to be conquered all over again. Gillespie had proved to be not only a martinet but had gone wild with his new authority. Two persons could not go about the streets of the Pueblo together, ordered Gillespie. There were to be no gatherings at home. A man could not gallop his horse through the streets. Shops must close at sundown. Liquor could not be sold without his permission. Houses were searched. Prominent townsmen were arrested and jailed on suspicion. To show Gillespie what they thought of all this, Los Angeles *señoritas* presented him with a basket of peaches—after the peaches had been rolled in cactus spines. Unhappiness, hostility, then revolt! Captain Flores was chosen *comandante general* of revolting, patriotic Angelenos, aided by José Antonio Carrillo and Andrés Pico. The camp of the patriots was Paredón Blanco, the heights—now Boyle Heights—east of the Los Angeles River. From this place a proclamation was issued, calling upon the citizens to arise and throw out the North American adventurers. Gillespie's garrison was surrounded. They held out for a few days in Pío Pico's old headquarters, then took a position on the hill

Abel Stearns' Main Street home, called El Palacio, was the social center of the Pueblo in the early 1850s. This photograph was taken about 1875 shortly before the adobe structure was torn down to make way for the Baker Block. *Courtesy of Title Insurance and Trust Company.*

dominating the Plaza. Soon they yielded to Flores' demands, but were graciously allowed to march out of Los Angeles with colors flying, drums beating, and to proceed to San Pedro. Santa Barbara and San Diego also were occupied by Flores' men.

For a while the *Californios* did well. Their plan was to wage guerrilla warfare and keep the Americans from getting to the interior. Flores was named interim governor. Fifty horsemen, under Carrillo, defeated the combined forces of Captain William Mervine—sent to San Pedro after Juan Flaco Brown's appeal—and those of Gillespie, which had not yet sailed. This fight took place on or near Rancho San Pedro and was featured by the repeated firing of a four-pounder, brass fieldpiece dragged to and fro with *reatas* attached to California saddles. *Californios* also inflicted a terrific defeat to the dragoons of General Stephen W. Kearny at San Pascual in present day San Diego County. Kearny had marched west from Santa Fé. At San Pascual the Californians, under Andrés Pico, rode fast horses and used with deadly effect their nine-foot, spear-pointed lances. The American survivors of San Pascual limped into San Diego, from which town Stockton had decided to

Bella Union Hotel, about the year 1871, when it was competing with the newer Pico House. The Bella Union was El Pueblo's pioneer hostelry. *Courtesy Title Insurance and Trust Company.*

[44]

attack Los Angeles. The rest was routine. The re-grouped forces of Stockton and Kearny marched north through what is now San Diego, Orange, and Los Angeles counties. Two minor engagements were fought—one on January 8, 1847, at Paso de Bartolo on the willow-lined San Gabriel River, and the other the next day at La Mesa on the Los Angeles River. Throughout Kearny's campaign, at San Pascual and later, Kit Carson, famous trapper and guide, played important roles.

On the morning of January 10, after receiving a verbal surrender from the lips of a committee sent out from Los Angeles, the men of Stockton and of Kearny marched into the Pueblo. All that day the band played in the Plaza, to the pleasure of the Californians, while soldiers, sailors, and marines celebrated with the local beverages.

Just north of the Plaza and in the lane that later became known as Olvera Street, a California boy had been guarding the home of Francisco Ávila's widow, Doña Encarnación Sepúlveda de Ávila. At that time an elbow of the house crossed the lane and formed its end. From this elbow occupants could watch Plaza events. With the approach of the Americans the widow Ávila had fled to the safer, but near-by home of a friend, vineyardist Don Luis Vignes. She had closed the doors and windows of her place and had left the young Californian to look after things. When the lad heard the brassy tunes of Stockton's band, however, he had to look out the window.

Baker Block, Corner of Main and Arcadia Streets, Los Angeles, Calif.

Plaza Church, Los Angeles, about 1885. *Courtesy Title Insurance and Trust Company.*

Plaza Church, Los Angeles, about 1885. *Courtesy Title Insurance and Trust Company.*

Then he walked out and ran to the Plaza. While he was enjoying the sights and sounds, staffmen of Stockton paused before the Ávila house, looked in the windows and saw the ample rooms and the attractive furniture. They promptly commandeered the place for Stockton's temporary home and headquarters. Many years later, as part of the celebration in 1931 of Los Angeles' 150th anniversary, a handsome descendant of Stockton and a charming descendant of the widow Ávila went through an amusing ceremony. The former apologized for Stockton's act. The girl, a professional dancer, accepted the apology and followed her acceptance with a superbly done, early California dance.

Meanwhile, Frémont with his buckskin battalion of 400 mounted riflemen had been marching south along the coast from Monterey. The day after Stockton and Kearny entered Los Angeles he entered San Fernando Valley and stopped at the Mission. The Californians had lost their interest in resistance and were quite willing to begin negotiations for a treaty of capitulation. Andrés Pico had succeeded Flores when the latter left for Sonora. Pico appointed José Antonio Carrillo and Agustin Olvera as treaty commissioners for the Californians. On the morning of January 13, 1847, Pico and Frémont signed the Treaty of Cahuenga. Their place of meeting and signature was the Cahuenga ranch house—its site today being at 3919 Lankershim Boulevard, in North Hollywood, directly

St. Vibiana's Cathedral near Second and Main Streets, 1886.

Sonoratown, Los Angeles, as delineated in 1886.

opposite the buildings of Universal City studios. This formally ended the California phase of the Mexican War. Actual cession of California to the United States by Mexico took place in the following year through the Treaty of Guadalupe Hidalgo.

In Los Angeles Frémont took full command, while Stockton and Kearny left for the north. Townsmen heard that Frémont had been appointed governor by Stockton and were convinced of the truth of the rumor when they saw him take over the largest house in the Pueblo for his headquarters. This was Captain Alexander Bell's two-story building—called Bell's Row, and later Mellus' Row—standing at the corner of Los Angeles and Aliso streets. From its balcony Frémont could inspect his troops garrisoned below.

Townsmen also saw work being resumed on the earthen fort atop the hill that rose above the Plaza. It had been started when Los Angeles was re-captured and was finished by members of the Mormon Battalion. These bearded young men, recruited at Mormon camps in Iowa, had volunteered for service in California. They reached the Pueblo in March, too late for the fighting, but in time for garrison duty and other useful activities. On July 4, 1847, everyone who was able climbed the hill to watch the American flag being raised over the completed fort. They heard Colonel Jonathan D. Stevenson make a dedication speech, naming the fort in memory of Captain Benjamin D. Moore, who lost his life in the battle of San Pascual. Angelenos today, standing on the Main Street side of the Plaza, can look up at what is left of Fort Moore Hill and see the huge sculptured panel or wall placed there and dedicated on July 4, 1958, as a memorial to pioneer troops and settlers.

Colonel Stevenson and his regiment of New York Volunteers had arrived in Los Angeles in May to take over the job of maintaining order. Frémont, always a controversial figure, had just left, leaving behind both friends and detractors. Presently the Mormon Battalion would be mustered out, many of the members leaving for Salt Lake City. For the most part Los Angeles accepted the change from Mexican to American administration and went its way undisturbed. *Rancheros* came into town for business and pleasure as usual. They and the townsmen continued the normal pastimes of dancing, singing, and gambling. Bullfights took place without interruption. Fiestas and church festivals were held as they had always been held. The *ayuntamiento* kept its functions, for the military had urged *alcaldes* and civil officers to continue regular activities. While the American soldiers occasionally clashed with civilians, many of them enjoyed the Pueblo's social life and added to the Pueblo's gaiety.

Within a year and a half, however, two events took place which made a profound change in Pueblo life. The first was the discovery of gold at Coloma in January of 1848, which in a few months drew thousands of Mexican miners from Sonora to the California gold fields, and which ultimately greatly enriched Southern California cattle raisers. Los Angeles was a way station for these Sonorans, who began to arrive long before the first wagons of American gold seekers could reach California. Some got no farther. In fact, so many Sonorans finally

Sonoratown, Los Angeles, looking north on Buena Vista Street, now North Broadway. About 1887.

settled in the oldest section of the Pueblo—the area that had drawn the founders—that it came to be called Sonoratown. Sonorans were followed by Americans taking southern routes from eastern states. Los Angeles, though several hundred miles from the mines, was vitally and increasingly affected by the Gold Rush. The second event to help change the Pueblo way of life was the mustering out of the New York Volunteers in September of 1848. This left Los Angeles streets filled with loafers—Sonorans and disbanded soldiers. There were many honorable young men among those who enlisted in New York with Stevenson. Others came from brawling Bowery and Five Points gangs who ended up as notorious California criminals. Presently, to the onlooker, the chief occupations in El Pueblo appeared to be gambling, drinking, carousing, and debauchery. "Monte banks, cockfights, and liquor shops are to be seen in all directions," wrote Dr. John S. Griffin in March of 1849 to his friend Colonel Stevenson, who was then in Monterey. "A Californian is a rare sight now on the streets. You never see them parading about on their fine horses as formerly." Once a street of happy homes, *Calle de los Negros*, opening into the Plazuela and the Plaza, was well on its way to becoming a pandemonium of races, gambling, vice, and crime. The whole character of the Plaza was infected, though thick walls gave much protection to the occupants of town houses. The timidity of the *Californios* in the presence of idle and vicious newcomers, it should be added, was somewhat temporary. They soon became the direct beneficiaries of the Gold Rush—with the rise in cattle prices—and as such were able to adjust themselves to the new situation and to enjoy their brawling Pueblo.

The town's treasury was empty. That was normal. When the Pueblo began to boom, however, the members of the *ayuntamiento* saw a way of keeping the treasury filled. That way was to go into the real estate business, for, as a Spanish Pueblo, Los Angeles was entitled to four square leagues of land, a princely patrimony. Under the rules of the military government in California, however, no land could be sold without reference to a map. Los Angeles had never been surveyed and Los Angeles had no surveyor. In the town's dilemma, Lieutenant E. O. C. Ord of the United States Army was assigned by the military government to help. His assistant was William Rich Hutton, who used his spare time to make drawings of Pueblo scenes. Together they mapped the heart of the Pueblo during the months of July and August, 1849. They used the church as their starting point and covered a large area north, south, east, and west of the Plaza. Streets were given

The front parlor or living room of Doña Arcadia Bandini de Baker's luxurious apartment in the Baker Block. *Courtesy Mrs. Arcadia Bandini Brennan.*

both their Spanish and English names: *Calle Principal*—Main Street; *Calle Primavera* — Spring Street; *Calle Fortin* — Fort Street (now Broadway); *Calle Loma* — Hill Street, etc. There was the Street of the Grasshoppers, Eternity Street, Bull Street, Short Street, Street of the Hornets, and Street of the Virgins. East of the occupied area was a pattern of cornfields and vineyards, while west were the hills. There were numbered blocks and numbered lots. The town's first auction of town lots was in November, when $2,490 was raised from bargain hunters. The newer district south of the Plaza brought the best prices. This auction set the pace—and Los Angeles never stopped exchanging its patrimony for cash until it had left, out of its four square leagues, the park spaces now called Pershing, Elysian, and Plaza; even the site of the present City Hall had to be bought back.

The transition in Los Angeles from Mexican to American government in 1850 was easy. A secret *junta* of prominent Angelenos met early in March in the Plaza home of Agustin Olvera, who the year before had been named "judge of the first instance" by Military Governor Riley. They drew up a slate of candidates for the new offices of the county government set up by the new American legislature. *Californios* were in the majority and at the election held April 1, the slate won. On April 4 Los Angeles was incorporated as an American city. A mayor was elected instead of an *alcalde*, and a council instead of an *ayuntamiento*. On September 9 California was admitted to the Union as a state, but this brought little immediate happiness to the southern *rancheros*, who feared they would be bearing new burdens of taxation.

Meanwhile Los Angeles townsmen and *rancheros* found themselves in an increasingly favorable position because of the enormous demand for beef cattle that had been started by the Gold Rush. Prices had begun to rise in 1849. Northern supplies were quickly exhausted. Southern California had had several seasons of good rains, and on the ranchos round about Los Angeles the grass was plentiful and the cattle many and fat. The cattle business paid better than mining. Soon the *rancheros* had more money than in their fondest dreams. For seven years cattle prices continued to rise and cattle drives north were a new feature of ranch living. It cost two to four dollars to get a steer north, but the steer brought $50 to $70, or higher, during the fall and winter of 1853 and 1854. Before the Gold Rush cattle were slaughtered only for hides, tallow, and dried beef, with hides worth two dollars each and tallow six to eight cents a pound.

A beautiful Chinese girl of the old Los Angeles Chinatown. *Courtesy Title Insurance and Trust Company.*

A street in old Chinatown, Los Angeles, east of Market Street. The tower of the red-brick Los Angeles High School seen on distant hilltop. Photo 1898. *Courtesy Title Insurance and Trust Company.*

With its new prosperity, El Pueblo went mad. Californians knew how to spend money. They bought fancy clothes, added second stories to their town houses on the Plaza, built bigger ranch homes, put on better horse races, and were heavy patrons of the gambling houses. They imported carriages, thousand-dollar shawls, and lace-curtained, four-poster bedsteads. Don José Sepúlveda and Don Vicente Lugo wore thousand-dollar suits, and their horses were equally resplendent. The money *Californios* spent did things to the shopkeepers, to the craftsmen in leather and silver, to the gamblers, to all the unsavory characters who came in for a share, and to the town itself.

Northern gamblers, outlaws, and prostitutes followed the money south. Some were driven out of San Francisco and northern towns and camps by vigilance committees. Race wars, too, aimed at Sonoran miners in the Mother Lode, started the bandit gangs of dark-skinned, embittered men who robbed and killed in all the southern counties. Los Angeles, close to the Mexican border, was their rallying place. The invaders lived close to the Plaza to ply their trades. Those lowest in the scale drifted into *Calle de los Negros,* popularly called "Nigger Alley," a place of discordant music, jingling gold, pistol shots, and the roar of the mob. The Golden Eagle—*La*

Store in old Los Angeles Chinatown, decorated for New Year's.
Courtesy Title Insurance and Trust Company.

Aguila de Oro—was one of the most notorious of its resorts,
where armed thugs guarded tables piled with gold, ready to
beat and kick into the filthy alley any patron who protested
being stripped of his wealth. Indians, fired with *aguardiente*,
would finish off such a victim. The more reputable gambling
places were also close to the Plaza but somewhat apart from
"the Alley." Los Angeles became the toughest and most law-
less city west of Santa Fé.

The Pueblo's most hardboiled characters were pointed out,
with pride, to the town's new arrivals—after they had been
given a tour of the dives and the gambling houses. It was not
hard to find Crooked Nose Smith, who had killed six men "up
north." Smith's promise to Los Angeles was that he would kill
no one there until just before he left for Mexico. He kept his
vow to the letter, killing a gambler the day before his depar-
ture. Cherokee Bob was another favorite sight on Los Angeles
streets. He was a killer, with a long record and a reputation for
never failing to get his man. Then there was an outlaw named
Urives, who attained distinction as a man of superhuman en-
durance. After being shot, stabbed, and stoned on the street,
on one occasion, he fought his way to his horse, with revolver
and bowie knife, mounted, and returned to scatter his enemies.
He then got his wounds bandaged, for he had been shot three

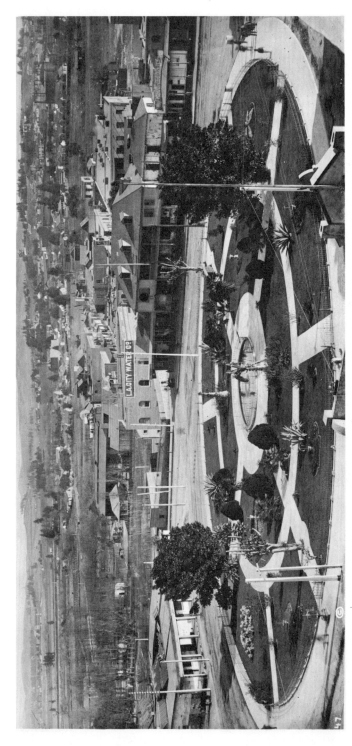

Los Angeles Plaza, 1890. Lugo House middle background. Olvera House background left. *Courtesy Title Insurance and Trust Company.*

times and stabbed till his clothes were almost cut from his body. Immediately afterward he rode up and down Main Street for an hour daring any gringo officer to arrest him. He was not arrested. If lucky, a newcomer might see the boss of the gamblers, Jack Powers, lording it over his followers. Powers had come to California as a soldier with Stevenson's New York Volunteers and then had gone in for "business" on his own. He was not only a gambler, but a cattle bandit, a killer, and a force up and down the state, with friends in high places. He looked like a gentleman, rode well, kept a string of race horses, and always surrounded himself with bodyguards.

To help stem the tide of crime and violence which in the 1850s resulted in daily killings, shootings, and stabbings in the streets of Los Angeles, a group of leading townsmen met in the El Dorado Saloon on Main Street one July day in 1853. Here they organized the Los Angeles Rangers, semi-vigilante, semi-social, made famous by Horace Bell in his *Reminiscences of a Ranger*. Other volunteer groups sprang up, with similar aims, as well as many spontaneous vigilante committees or mobs. The Ranger group is said to have brought about the execution of twenty-two men in 1854 and 1855. In addition, there were scores of outright lynchings, sometimes with racial feelings dominant. In spite of the activities of these volunteer police and mobs, crime was rampant for two decades, climax-

Pico House and stages, about 1875. *Courtesy Title Insurance and Trust Company.*

ing in the bloody pogrom of 1871 when a mob murdered more than a score of Chinese in the Plaza area.

Life in the 1850s was difficult for *rancheros* whose town houses rubbed shoulders with *Calle de los Negros*, with gambling houses, and with grog shops. It was not like life in the simple 1830s or 1840s, filled with fiestas, bullfights, and dances. Of course *rancheros* and their families could stay on their ranchos, and some did. Others threatened to move to Mexico. But Los Angeles offered fun as well as danger, and town house walls were thick and the windows were barred and could be barricaded.

Don Abel Stearns, merchant and *ranchero*, who owned more Southern California land than anyone else, had an embarrassing adventure at this time. His large, massive-walled Main Street home, within a short distance of the Plaza and called *El Palacio*, was the social center of Los Angeles. It was presided over by his lovely young wife, who before marriage was Arcadia Bandini of a prominent California family. The occasion was a Washington's Birthday ball given in 1853 in the hundred-foot ballroom. Two or three of the guests were professional gamblers. Gamblers not invited decided to break up the party. They used a cannon and a battering ram and when the dancing was at its height crashed through a door leading into the *sala*. The first man to enter was stopped with a bullet

Tallyho Stage at Pico House, 1884, to pick up passengers for the "Grand Round," Pasadena, Sunnyside, Sierra Madre, Santa Anita, San Gabriel Mission and back. *Courtesy Title Insurance and Trust Company.*

Pico House dining room, with glimpse of courtyard. *Photo by A. C. Varela. Courtesy State Division of Beaches and Parks.*

by the dancer nearest the door. The firing became general, but finally the raiders were beaten back into the street.

The more normal activities of the Stearns household, continuing even into the American period, were a delight to a neighbor and half-brother of Doña Arcadia, the scholarly Don Arturo Bandini. "Here," writes Susanna Bryant Dakin in her introduction to Bandini's *Navidad*, "Don Arturo could observe the daily pageant of 'adobe days'—silver-saddled horses suddenly reined-in before the *patio* entrance, calico-padded *carretas* carrying those who were too young or too old or too fat to ride, bringing country cousins or sea captains or grey-robed *padres* to visit the childless Stearns household. Within high *adobe* walls, Indian servants were continually at work—preparing for a gala dinner, an evening *baile*, or an afternoon *cha* served from a huge silver service. Laughter, chatter, snatches of song reached Don Arturo in his study, even while he regretted an invitation from Doña Arcadia because of a letter to write, a book to read."

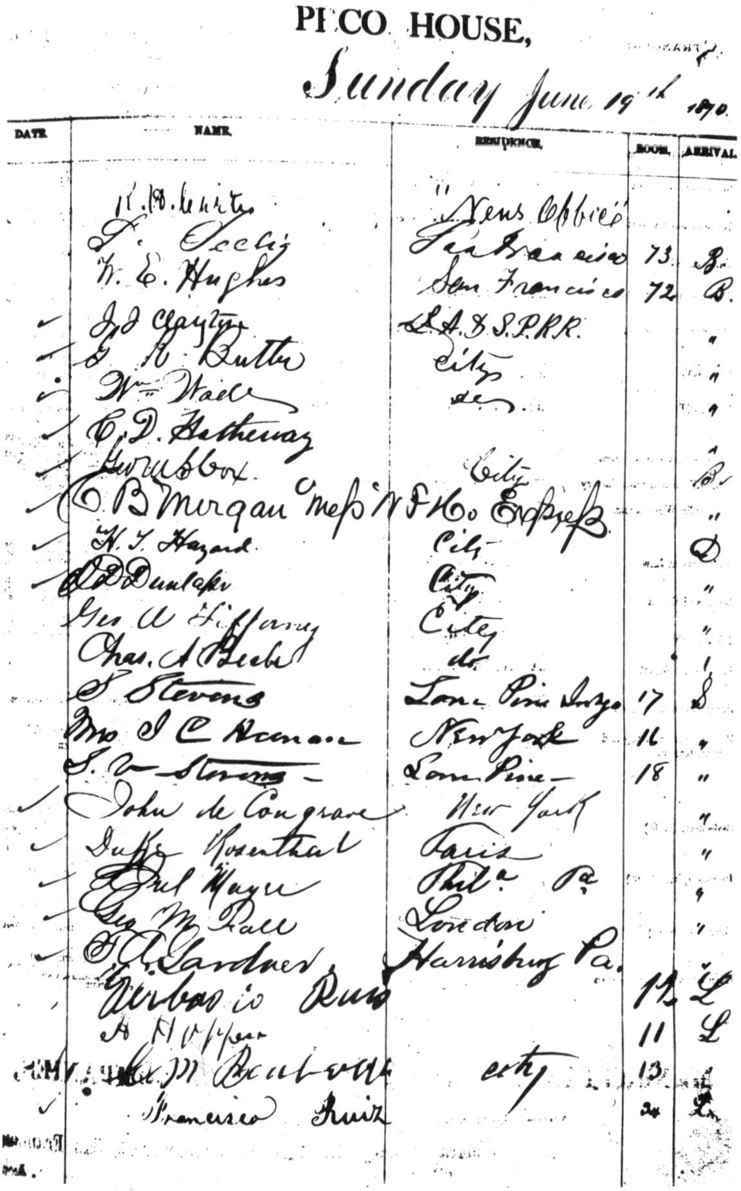

PICO HOUSE,

Sunday June 19th 1870

DATE	NAME	RESIDENCE	ROOM	ARRIVAL

The Pico House opened June 19, 1870. Here is the first page of the hotel's register. *Courtesy Los Angeles County Museum, History Division.*

Laura Garfias de Lainesse, a member of the Ávila family, one of the daughters of the widow Ávila married Don Manuel Garfias, soldier and owner of Rancho San Pascual. The Ávila home with its fifteen rooms, was large enough to house members of the two families. *Courtesy Christine Sterling.*

Both Bandini and Harris Newmark recall that even in the 1850s—when Los Angeles had been invaded by motley hordes —the Plaza was still the scene of old-time festivities. The *Corpus Christi* processions were never more resplendent and were enjoyed by newcomers as well as *Californios*. The old families still erected altars in front of their Plaza homes and decorated them with silks, satins, laces, even jewelry. The last play of the *Pastores*, as recalled by Bandini, took place in the Plaza on

Patio in rear of Avila House before it was transformed into a garden. This adobe was erected possibly as early as 1818. *Courtesy Title Insurance and Trust Company.*

Pico House, Merced Theatre, and Masonic Lodge, from left to right, as they appeared in the early 1870s. *Courtesy Security-First National Bank.*

Christmas eve of 1861. *Rancheros* and townsmen patronized the numerous booths that had been set up for the occasion. The air was filled with the cries of the vendors of *tamales, enchiladas, tortillas,* candy, and fruit, as well as with the twanging of guitars, the shrieking of violins, and the voices of singers.

Rancho days in the Los Angeles area, as elsewhere in California, practically ended in the 1860s. The ownership of the ranchos passed from *Californio* hands to American, almost without exception. This did not happen overnight. The boom of the Fifties had ended in 1857 when the flush era in the gold mines was over and when the demand and prices for Southern California beef dropped. Most of the *rancheros* had overspent themselves and were in debt. Their land was blanketed with mortgages on which they paid fantastically high interest rates. Townsmen were hard hit, too. Even the gambling houses were deserted, and the gamblers and outlaws were getting out as fast as they came in. Bullfights were infrequent. In the midst of all this, *Californio* land claimants were still trying to prove to Federal commissioners and courts that they were the actual owners of the ranchos they had occupied so long. Under the

Plaza Church, Los Angeles, about 1889. *Courtesy Title Insurance and Trust Company.*

The Los Angeles Plaza, as depicted in Ward Bros. brochure, "Souvenir of Los Angeles and Vicinity," published in 1886. Pico House and hill-top homes in the background.

Land Act of 1851, which set up a Land Commission, the Government was attempting to segregate privately owned land from public domain. This involved years of delay, continuous expense, squatter troubles, and the depression of values of ranch land which—with unproved titles—the *rancheros* could not subdivide or sell. On top of these difficulties a series of drought years set in, beginning with 1862, which brought final ruin to the *rancheros*. They were either foreclosed or they were compelled to deed or partition their lands for the benefit of creditors. The pastoral age ended, cattle no longer grazed the plains, and the ranchos, American owned, were largely broken up and offered for sale as farm acreage.

In the heart of the Pueblo—if Los Angeles could even then be referred to as a Pueblo—the character and the personnel of the Plaza changed. The town houses had new owners and new tenants. A growing Chinatown was pressing on the east. Vice interests were finding footholds in buildings and areas that had once been the pride of the Pueblo and of the *rancheros* roundabout. Don Ygnacio del Valle in 1861 moved back to his ranch, "Camulos," part of the original Rancho San Francisco. His Plaza home ultimately became a part of the colorful and bizarre Chinatown which during the 1860s and 1870s had arisen on the area that sloped east from the Plaza and that took in the land now occupied by the Union Station, its trackage and appurtenances. Don Vicente Lugo, former Beau Brummel of the Pueblo, vacated his town house and presented it to the parish priest. It became a boys' school in 1865 and finally St. Vincent's College, predecessor of Loyola University. When the college sought a better neighborhood, the Lugo house became an interesting segment of the Chinese quarter and in its last days the property of the Hop Sing Tong. Judge Olvera was an active figure in the Pueblo until his death in the middle Seventies. The Olvera house became more and more dilapidated, falling into ruin and razed in 1917. Don Pío Pico, who had gone to Mexico at the outset of the Mexican War, had quickly returned to his beloved California to build a new home on his "Ranchita"—Rancho Paso de Bartolo—in the Whittier region. There he spent much of his time until, in 1869, he returned to the Plaza to make a final effort at its rehabilitation through the construction of a great hotel on the site of the home of Don José Antonio Carrillo, who had died in 1862. The adobe gambling house that once faced the Plaza became the property of John G. Downey, a newcomer and druggist who became a great landowner and a governor of California. It was presently acquired by an Englishman, John

Jones, in whose family (Jones-Simpson) it remained—as a tree-shrouded residence—until recent years. Francisco O'Campo, once wealthy, no longer watched cockfights in his front yard. "In his later years," commented Newmark, "he used to sit on the curbstone near the Plaza, a character, quite forlorn, utterly dejected in appearance, and despondently recalling the bygone days of his prosperity." Through all these years, however, and to the present day, the buff-colored church continued to dominate the Plaza and to serve the ever-changing people of the area, its bells calling to the faithful and to the unfaithful.

The Americans really took over the Pueblo.

Campo Santo, at the end of Eternity Street, was the final destination of most of the townsmen of El Pueblo. Even Campo Santo itself is no more. *Photo by Charles Puck. Courtesy Title Insurance and Trust Company.*

Lucie Banning, age 15, belle of Los Angeles society in the 1890s, whose hill-top home looked out over the plaza.

V

Passing of "El Pueblo"

LONG BEFORE 1870 all signs pointed to a shift southward of Los Angeles' business, residential, and social center. Furthermore, the Plaza area itself had become "questionable." To use the language of the Los Angeles *Star*, the streets above and about the Plaza, especially Bath Street (now North Main), were "notoriously infested with shameless bawds."

Two notable efforts, nevertheless, were made to rehabilitate the original heart of the Pueblo—one by an eminent *Californio* and the other by a man from Indiana married to a California woman. In 1869-70 a palatial hotel was erected at the corner of Main Street and the Plaza, and in the latter half of 1870 the Merced Theater was built next to it on Main. The builder of the first was Don Pío Pico, who in his career summed up the Spanish, Mexican, and American periods in California's history and whose official life had centered in the Plaza. The builder of the theater was William Abbott, who had come to Los Angeles in 1853, had started a store close to the Plaza handling furniture and undertaking, and had married Mercedes García, who was a harpist, vocalist, and teacher of music, embroidery, and fine sewing at the school of the Sisters of Charity.

In July of 1869 Pico sold his interest in San Fernando Valley —Rancho Ex-Mission de San Fernando—for $115,000. The Carrillo house on the Plaza—scene of secret conferences and social gatherings—was on the market and had been since Carrillo's death in 1862. Don Pío made the decision to buy the corner and to erect there a hotel that would be the pride of Los Angeles.

Ground was broken in September of 1869 and the Carrillo tiled adobe crumbled to dust beneath the blows of workmen, causing much local comment on the passing of old landmarks. As built, the three-story Pico House was "American Romanesque, with deep-set arched doors and windows, slightly ponderous, and sturdy; the brick face was stuccoed and painted in imitation of light blue granite." The quotation is from Walter E. Rothman, who made close study of the hotel and its history for the Los Angeles County Museum's *Quarterly* of Summer, 1950. The building had a frontage of about 120 feet on Main by 95 on the Plaza. It had stone foundations, a cellar, brick walls, strong supporting beams, and a roof of tin, with heavy cornices. Its entrance was on Main Street. This opened on a high lobby with a double staircase leading to a mirrored landing ornamented with statues and vases. The staircase continued to a second-floor parlor. Connected with the lobby was a center court with a fountain. Birds sang in cages and flowers grew in baskets set in the surrounding corridors. To the right of the entrance-way was the office, with its bell wires and speaking tubes, and an adjoining reading room. There was a luxurious bar that could be entered from Main Street or the Plaza. The chandelier-lit dining rooms, one for families, the other for general guests, faced the Plaza and offered a view of its circular garden and central fountain, and also of the church. The kitchen, featured by hot-water tanks, faced Sanchez Street. There was a barber shop and a billiard room. Wells, Fargo & Company had an express office on the ground floor.

The furnishings of the Pico House were sumptuous: heavy velvet or Brussels carpets; prints and paintings on the walls; lounges, arm chairs, and sofas in green and gold, a carved walnut wardrobe for each bedroom; lace curtains; and for the bridal suite rosewood furniture. The dining rooms were furnished with "small tables after the style of the Cosmopolitan in San Francisco." The building was gas-lit throughout. On the second and third floors there were "bathrooms and water closets for both sexes, convenient of access and approachable in the strictest privacy"—to quote from the detailed description appearing in the Los Angeles *Daily News* of May 25, 1870.

A distinguished staff, headed by the affable Don Antonio Cuyas, took care of the first guests, who arrived Sunday, June 19, 1870. Don Antonio was the former proprietor of the Barcelona Hotel in New York. His aides included Mr. George Pridham, erstwhile obliging clerk at the Bella Union, Mr. J. H. Gregory, popular bartender, and "French Charlie" Laugier, an accomplished cook and caterer whose reputation "extended from New Orleans to Los Angeles." Twenty-five guests signed the register that first day.

For ten years the Pico House fulfilled the hopes of Don Pío. It was the outstanding hotel and was the social and cultural

Feeding-the-dragon ceremony in Los Angeles' old Chinatown, which occupied the site of the present Union Station. *Courtesy Title Insurance and Trust Company.*

The opening, in September, 1884, of the new engine house of 38's Engine Company No. 1 facing the Plaza from the south side. The name of the company was derived from the fact that there were 38 members when it was reorganized in 1874. This building, at No. 26 Plaza Street, later received a bell which was hung on top of the roof. It functioned as an engine house until late in 1897. *Photo courtesy State Division of Beaches and Parks.*

center of Los Angeles. This was true even though Pico himself during that period suffered one financial disaster after another, with law suit following law suit. The register of the hotel carried such well-known names as Ávila, Sepúlveda, del Valle, Carrillo, Dominguez, Lugo, Rowland, Lankershim, Wolfskill, Hellman, Flint, and Bixby, and such individuals as General Stoneman, Charles Nordhoff, Colonel R. S. Baker and his wife Arcadia de Baker, Helen Hunt Jackson, Madame Helena Modjeska, and a host of other celebrities.

The Pico House had surpassed and overshadowed the earlier Bella Union, the Lafayette, and the United States Hotel. In its turn it would be succeeded and outdistanced by hostelries built farther southward in the area that finally left the Plaza behind in shabby isolation.

Shortly after the opening of the Pico House Mr. and Mrs. William Abbott ordered excavation work started on a building adjoining that would be just a few feet higher than Pico's. Mrs. Abbott— Doña Mercedes—furnished most of the capital. The land they bought for this purpose had originally been the site of the El Dorado Saloon, which flourished in a two-story frame building that had been brought—pre-fabricated—around the Horn. The proprietor of this popular drinking spot, according to Major Horace Bell, was "an elegant Irishman" named John Hughes, "a scholar," "a splendid gentleman" and a "good judge of whiskey." The lower floor was a bar and billiard room, the upper floor was used for sleeping quarters. In 1853 the El Dorado was transformed into a Methodist church, with the Reverend Adam Bland as its minister. Bland tore down Hughes' sign and started Los Angeles' first Protestant church. Hughes never recovered from the shock. Meanwhile, William Abbott had done better with his furniture and undertaking than Adam Bland had with his preaching. By 1863 he needed new quarters and was able to buy the Methodist Church property. The Abbotts' plan was to build a three-story brick structure on that site, to be flanked on the north by the Pico House and on the south by the two-story brick Masonic Temple which had been erected in 1858. This would take care of the store on the first floor, provide a theater on the second, and family living quarters on the third. Within six months the building was completed. Like the Pico House it extended back from Main to Sanchez.

The iron balcony of the Merced was designed so that a band could play there before performances. A stairway led to the theater on the second floor—to which, ultimately, there was a private entrance from the Pico House for the use of its guests.

There was a drop curtain, on which was painted an Italian landscape, according to Sue Wolfer Earnest, who wrote an excellent dissertation on the history of the theater in Southern California for the University of Southern California and to whom we are indebted for a complete list of all the productions at the Merced Theater from its opening in January, 1871. Drapes were of red plush edged with gold fringe. There was a 35 by 25 foot stage, two dressing rooms, and four boxes. When a balcony was added—later—an audience of upwards of four hundred people could be accommodated.

The Merced was christened on New Year's Eve, 1870, with a concert and ball. Drum Barracks at Wilmington furnished a band and the music. Leading citizens, including Pío Pico, Judge Ygnacio Sepúlveda, and John R. Downey formed the committee in charge of the important event. Private boxes, reported Miss Earnest, were $5 and $10, orchestra chairs $1.50, parquet $1. For the occasion Judge H. K. S. O'Melveny made an address which the *Star* said was received with "unbounded applause."

Professionally speaking, the Merced Theater began its life on January 30 following. A dramatic company of twenty-four players, headed by Kitty Blanchard and McKee Rankin and sponsored by Thomas Maguire of San Francisco, began a ten-day engagement. Handbills in Spanish and in English advertised the event. The first attraction offered was *Fanchon, the Cricket.* This opening performance was highly praised by the *Star*, which concluded its comment by reporting that "the house was crowded with a fashionable audience, the music was good, the arrangements complete, the actors were well received, and loudly applauded, and the whole affair was a pronounced success, the audience separating delighted with the elegant entertainment."[7]

The same company put on sure-fire favorites like *The Colleen Bawn*, *Rip Van Winkle*, and *Anthony and Cleopatra*, while Miss Blanchard did mouth-organ solos between acts.

Then followed the California Minstrels, Carter's dramatic company, Nathan Juveniles, Frank M. Bates' dramatic company, Johnny Allen's burlesque, and a procession of other professionals in engagements of various lengths.

Attendance did not hold up well; this was blamed by the press on poor acoustics, the clatter on uncarpeted stairs, and the noise made by the Abbott children scurrying on stairways and landing.

[7]Howard Swan, *Music in the Southwest* (San Marino, The Huntington Library, 1952).

Since the days of hide-trading San Pedro was the port for El Pueblo and surrounding ranchos. In the 1850s competing stage lines carried passengers and freight between Los Angeles and the sea.

Bell's Row, built for Captain Alexander Bell at the corner of Aliso and Los Angeles Streets, became Mellus' Row when bought by Francis Mellus. Frémont used it in 1847 as his headquarters.

"Old man Abbott, thin and of rather nervous temperament, always more or less unshaven," wrote newspaperman William A. Spaulding, "was apt to be in attendance somewhere about the premises, busy about one thing or another, and Mrs. Abbott, a middle-aged Spanish woman, of dominating presence, sometimes appeared and took command of the children."

The theater was closed for nearly a year, during which time—and later—improvements were made: armchairs were substituted for rough seats, the scenery was repainted, the walls and floors were cleaned, lighting and ventilation were bettered, a balcony was added, and a saloon was opened downstairs.

Small-time companies, troupes that specialized in visiting "interior" towns, continued to play the Merced, with heavy emphasis on melodramas. Popular productions included *The Lady of Lyons, East Lynne, Camille, Uncle Tom's Cabin,* and *Ten Nights in a Bar Room.* Minstrel shows occasionally packed the house.

By 1875 the life of the Merced "as a first class show-house" was over. "Now began its long progressive deterioration," wrote Miss Earnest, "both in type and quality of performances, and in audience."

Following the last appearance of the Original Georgia Minstrels, in June of 1876, the Merced became Wood's Opera House. J. H. Wood took it over and featured melodramas, with drinks served during the performances. Then he made it strictly a variety house. Friday was "Ladies' Night," and shows were changed weekly. Boxing, wrestling bouts, and naughty farces spiced the fare. Harris Newmark described this so-called opera house as "a typical Western song and dance resort, the gallery being cut up into boxes where the actresses between acts mingled with the crowd; patrons indulged in drinking and smoking, and the bar in front did a thriving business." A visitor in Los Angeles at this time reported that the streets were at the peak of their activity in the evenings, "especially at the entrance to the opera-house where there is so much pushing and shouting going on that it is difficult to get through."

The hollow boom of a cannon mounted on a platform in front of Wood's Opera House shook Main Street shortly after the noon hour on September 5, 1876. It told the crowds choking the flag-decorated street that railroad connection with San Francisco—and therefore with the nation—had that moment been established. Most Angelenos on that day had milled the streets or crowded the saloons while waiting for this announcement that the city's long fight to get the Southern Pacific to come south from San Francisco had ended in success. Other gaily-garbed and specially-favored citizens, 355 of them, watched the final spike-driving ceremonies at the station of Lang in Soledad Canyon, 43 miles away. The golden spike, fashioned by a Los Angeles jeweler, was driven home by Charles Crocker—one of the "Big Four" of the Southern Pacific—who delivered six hefty blows with a silver hammer. This spike joined the two sections of the Southern Pacific, one working south, one north, and united Los Angeles and San Francisco. Telegraphic announcement went to Wood's Opera House and to the world. It was the culmination of the wishes of Angelenos, expressed in 1872 when they went to the polls and voted to meet the Southern Pacific's subsidy demands in order to avoid being bypassed. It was perhaps Los Angeles' most significant moment, for it ended El Pueblo's isolation and was the first step in opening Los Angeles to the world.

In spite of this happy participation in a great event, Wood's Opera House continued on the downward path, and in June of 1878 the owner, J. H. Wood, was bankrupt. Thereafter the building served for a while as the Armory for the Los Angeles Guards, then in 1883 as the Club Theater, a variety house,

The Plaza served as a wholesale market in the 1890s. Judge Olvera's one-time home shown in right rear partly hidden by tree. *Courtesy Audio-Visual Section, Los Angeles City Schools.*

The winery of pioneer vineyardist Jean Louis Vignes, purchased and taken over in 1855 by two nephews named Sainsevain. The large tree shown is El Aliso, a landmark since Indian days.

operated by the Perry Brothers. Leon J. Rose, Jr. recalls taking John L. Sullivan there in the fall of that year and having fun showering the Stanley Sisters, a local pair, with silver dollars thrown from their box. The entertainment continually degenerated, however, until a ball given there in June, 1887, was described by the Los Angeles *Times* as a "prostitute's carnival."

One other building, a block south of Wood's Theater, calls for brief mention for it had a direct tie-in with Pueblo days and also helped delay the move of the town's business center to First Street and beyond. Shortly after the coming of the railroad Don Abel Stearns' *Palacio* on Main Street was demolished to make way for the handsome, three-story Baker Block. Stearns had died in 1871 and his widow, Doña Arcadia, married Colonel R. S. Baker, a man of wealth and ideas, who in 1877 began the destruction of the famous adobe—scene of his wife's social triumphs—and the construction of Los Angeles' outstanding business building. During its construction Colonel and Mrs. Baker were guests of the Pico House. The Baker Block, California's "most elegant structure outside of San Francisco," remained the center of Los Angeles' retail trade for many years and its suites long drew the more affluent attorneys of the town and some of the leading citizens, including the widow Baker, who had a luxurious apartment there. Today its site is largely occupied by the rushing chasm of the Hollywood Freeway.

When Los Angeles got its transcontinental rail connections in 1876 the Pueblo chapter in its story ended and the modern chapter began. A more direct connection with the east was established in 1881, when the Southern Pacific completed construction work between Los Angeles and El Paso. Henceforth the story of Los Angeles is one of newcomers constantly pouring into its expanding area, an influx that continued year by year, resulting in early agricultural development, especially citrus, and the rise of tributary communities. This modern phase is punctuated by real estate booms in 1887, 1906, 1923, and 1946—the most fantastic being that of the Eighties, though the 1920s brought a greater mass migration of human beings from all over the United States seeking climate and opportunities. Meanwhile, Los Angeles in 1892 discovered that it was sitting on a fat reservoir of oil. In 1909 it acquired the harbor at San Pedro and transformed it into one of the important ports of the world. In the years after 1910 the Hollywood area became famous for the making of movies. In 1913 Los Angeles began to import water from Owens Valley, later from Mono Basin and still later, in 1941, from the Colorado River—insuring that the city would live. In 1941-45, as a part of World War II activities, the industrial phase of the city and county really began—and with it more people, more automobiles, smog (first noted in 1943), huge expansion of aerial travel, and freeway development.

The old ranchos that once ringed the Pueblo, bearing Spanish names that today recall the pastoral age, gave way to farms, communities, cities, re-subdivision, and finally to a continuous population area that now spreads over the coastal region of two counties and that may well soon sweep uninterruptedly from Santa Barbara to the Mexican border. Even the hills that rise to the rear and to the west of the Plaza were crowned in the 1870s, the 1880s, and the 1890s with Victorian and ornate homes of the well-to-do—offering a view of orange groves, gardens, orchards, and vineyards. In recent years these homes —as part of a substandard area—began to give way to freeway, Civic Center and Bunker Hill development projects. By the 1890s few of the picturesque characters of rancho days were still living. One of the last to go was Pío Pico, who died penniless in 1894. Even into the early 1890s visitors to the Plaza and Chinatown might see the stocky, jewelry-laden figure of this old man seated in front of the hotel which he had built in 1869 and which then was playing second fiddle to newer, better located hotels.

From the Plaza the town's social, business and cultural center had moved southward and westward, with new regional centers springing up all over the landscape—until frequently it was said of Los Angeles that, like Pirandello's play, *Six Characters in Search of an Author*, it was a series of suburbs seeking a city. Today the binding force of freeways and the rise of the ambitious group of Civic Center buildings at the intersection of Hollywood and Harbor freeways create and re-establish a new administrative center for the whole Los Angeles area. Its location is on old Pueblo land and it is close to the old Pueblo center at the Plaza.

While Los Angeles was pressing out in all directions, the small section in which it was born grew increasingly shabby and increasingly isolated. Much of Sonoratown with its continuous rows of small one-story adobe buildings had provided homes for Mexican-Americans who came in a never-ending stream. Presently the Mexican-Americans sought homes farther away. As adobe structures there or on the Plaza fell into disrepair or ruin, they were replaced with frame or brick business buildings. Growers of vegetables and fruit used the Plaza in the 1890s for a wholesale market, but Charles F. Lummis' Landmarks Club prevented this use from being more than temporary. Exotic Chinatown, occupying a close-packed area on both sides of Los Angeles and Alameda streets, year in and year out offered color, gaiety, and mystery to visitors and a place and way of life for Chinese. Then Chinatown bowed before the construction of a widely-spread Union Station—ready in the Spring of 1939—and its huge pattern of railroad lines. The Chinese moved to points farther north or farther south in Los Angeles. The doors of tolerated vice, flourishing since the days of *Calle de los Negros*, were rudely padlocked in 1909. That was the year of the triumph of municipal reform—part of a state-wide movement. By the 1920s there was only a scattered handful of original adobe homes left from rancho days. The "rich bench of earth" where Los Angeles had been born was then a drab and decaying miscellany broken only by occasional bohemian and Chinese restaurants enjoying cheap rental space and by the dark cluster of trees that marked the Plaza with its enduring church.

Looking toward Don Ygnacio Coronel's adobe home—in the days of its dilapidation—with old Calle de los Negros on right and extending north. Early 1870s, just before the extension of Los Angeles Street swept all before it. Lafayette Hotel stage in front. *Courtesy of Huntington Library.*

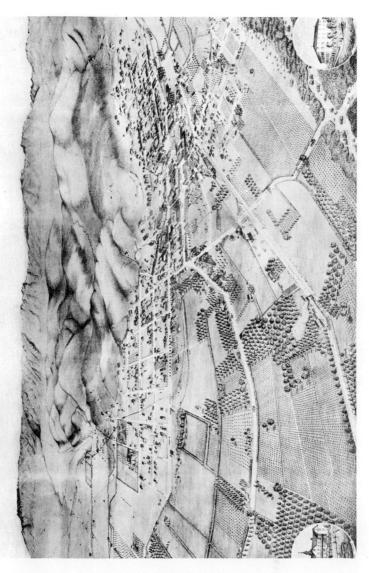

Los Angeles, 1871, a birdseye view as drawn by Augustus Koch. Plaza and business section upper right. In the foreground cornfields, vineyards, and orchards. *Lithographed by Britton & Rey.*

VI

Los Angeles Remembers its Past

ONE JANUARY MORNING IN 1928 a small, blue-eyed, red-haired woman named Christine Sterling was wandering about the Los Angeles Plaza. She walked along Olvera Street, then a filthy alley with sewage running down the middle gutter, a slum and crime center. She came to a sudden stop when she reached the forlorn Ávila House. In front of it was a condemnation sign put there by the city!

For nearly two years Mrs. Sterling, San Francisco-born and of English descent, had been working on her pet idea—the conversion of the old Plaza into a Latin-American social and commercial center. She had been fascinated by the historical Spanish-Mexican background of Los Angeles ever since she had come to the city with her two children and had pioneered Chavez Ravine as a low-cost residential area. She had fallen in love with the Mexican-Americans who had followed her example and had helped transform the arroyos and slopes of the Ravine into a pleasant and colorful community close to the Sonoratown of early days. She had gone to Harry Chandler, publisher of the *Times*. He had pronounced her Plaza rejuvenation idea a "great project" and had asked John McGroarty, California historian and author of the popular *Mission Play*, to write it up for the Sunday *Times*. "The Plaza Beautiful" duly appeared and there were meetings, much talk, and attempts at fund-raising. By 1928, however, the pet project was in the doldrums and Mrs. Sterling wrote in her diary that the "boat was foundering." What she needed, without realizing it, was a dramatic incident to wake up townsmen to the importance of their city's historic past. The condemnation sign in front of the dilapidated adobe structure, which was perhaps Los Angeles' oldest surviving residence and which had served as Commodore Stockton's headquarters in 1847, furnished the incident. She wrote in her diary: "I found the answer to all my problems by looking at its neglect. If this old

Homes on Bunker Hill rising above the area of El Pueblo. A mighty redevelopment project, adjoining the Civic Center and Pueblo de Los Angeles State Historical Monument, takes them all. *Photo by George Figureida.*

Olvera Street, Los Angeles.
Union Pacific Railroad Photo.

Displaying his wares in Olvera Street, Los Angeles. *Union Pacific Railroad Photo.*

house, a century old, a definite tangible thing, which belonged to the history of Los Angeles was condemned to be destroyed, how could I, offering just conversation, hope to survive?"

Mrs. Sterling hunted up the owners of the Ávila House. They were members of the Rimpau family, grandchildren and great-grandchildren of the builder, Francisco Ávila. A daughter of the widow Ávila had married a German pioneer, Theodore Rimpau, and the Rimpau family had long occupied that portion of the adobe that still survives. In more recent years—out of sentiment alone—they had kept the burdensome building standing. Because of its deplorable condition, it had been condemned by the city. "Let me take this old place," Mrs. Sterling asked. The Rimpaus gave her a key and she paid a nominal rent.

Mrs. Sterling made a signboard ten feet high and twelve feet long. "Why Should This Be Condemned!" was the big-lettered heading. Beneath that, the adobe's history. She carried it in an express wagon and put it up alongside the city's sign.

Again Mrs. Sterling went to the publisher of the *Times* and also to the publishers of the *Examiner* and the *Herald-Express*. "Send your reporters to Olvera Street," she pleaded. They went, and the story of the Ávila House was blazoned in the newspapers.

Florence Dodson Schoneman of the Sepúlveda family, which formerly owned Rancho Los Palos Verdes, was the first to respond to the appeal for help in restoration. Through her efforts, and in good time, a grand piano from the old rancho was installed in one of the living rooms of the Ávila House. In fact, Mrs. Schoneman furnished a whole room with Sepúlveda family possessions. Essential repairs were made. Ultimately the thick-walled adobe became delightfully furnished in the manner and spirit of early California. The patio in the rear developed into a charming tree-and-vine-dominated garden where wild doves nested and raised their young. State-owned today and open to the public, this "haven of tranquility"—to use Ed Ainsworth's phrase—is visited by thousands of tourists. The Ávila House symbolizes and stimulates the rehabilitation of Olvera Street and the whole Plaza area.

But this is getting ahead of the story. Having appealed for help in saving the Ávila House, Mrs. Sterling went to the City Council. The gentlemen agreed to forget condemnation and furnished a gang of prison labor to clean up Olvera Street. Mrs. Sterling needed $25,000. Harry Chandler led off with $5,000 and got his friends to go along for the rest.

The movement to save and restore the Ávila House was

Union Station, Los Angeles, opened in April, 1939, on site of old Chinatown east of Plaza. *Union Pacific Railroad Photo.*

only a small part of a much larger program which started with the incorporation of "Plaza de Los Angeles." The board of directors was composed of fifteen leading Angelenos, starting off alphabetically with Chandler and ending with Sterling. Their announced purpose was "to preserve the Plaza as a monument to the founding of Los Angeles," and to create "an important Latin-American trade and social center," as well as tourist attraction. To make Olvera Street a "Latin-American street" and a "picturesque Mexican market place" was the first step. These purposes obviously had both spiritual and business values. Public-spirited citizens interested in the preservation of the city's historical background were invited to subscribe to stock in the corporation.

Out of this organized effort came first of all the transformation of Olvera Street into a gay, amusing, and—to children—enchanting Mexican village thoroughfare. It was done quickly, for it had the backing not only of prominent townsmen but of the Mexican-Americans also—Los Angeles having the largest Spanish-speaking population of any North American city outside of Mexico City. Today it is part of the state historical monument and is run by an organization called El Pueblo de Los Angeles—successor to Plaza de Los Angeles—the managing director of which is Christine Sterling. From the Ávila House at 14 Olvera Street she directs the operation not only of this thoroughfare, the shops and booths of which support from 300 to 400 Mexican-American families, but a much wider state-owned area near the Plaza.

Two million visitors each year are drawn to Olvera Street, now completely self-supporting from rental money paid by concessionaires. These visitors saunter by the shops lining its sides and the canopied booths that occupy its center. Both shops and booths are lively with color—red, blue, yellow, orange, and green—all faded to nice hues. The booths display strings and baskets of painted *maracas* (gourd rattles), *piñatas* in the form of pink donkeys, roosters, swans, and sheep, enormous and gaudy bank-bulls, big straw hats, *huaraches* (Mexican shoes), and hand-painted skirts. Some shops are large stores, to be entered by stairways that lead up or down, carrying Mexican importations. Over all is the spicy smell that comes from perfumed candles and open-air kitchens preparing food for al fresco eaters. There are silver and leather-work shops, shops that handle jewelry, pottery, Spanish records, nuts, and cigarets from all over the world. Others have such sweets as candied cactus, chocolate fudge, peanut pralines, and pumpkin candy. The tourist may watch candle-makers, work-

Los Angeles City Hall and Federal Building seen from the Union Station, all built on Pueblo land and close to the Plaza. *Union Pacific Railroad Photo.*

ers in glass, and a blacksmith. He may rest on a bench beneath a pepper or a palm tree. Theaters come and go. Sometimes there are street musicians. Restaurants are many, usually small, like the popular Anita's. The best known and the largest are La Golondrina, in the old Pelanconi Building, and El Paseo Inn, almost directly across the way. Both have colorful sidewalk tables, Mexican entertainment, tasty Mexican food, and Mexican drinks. La Golondrina is the oldest and is presided over by Señora Consuelo Castillo de Bonzo, who has contributed to the liveliness and popularity of the Street since its reactivation, whose Christmas parties are famous, and who participates in all the activities that are bringing the Plaza area into full life. The long-time proprietor of El Paseo Inn is María Elena Peluffo, who emphasizes nightly entertainment as well as good food. Olvera Street never misses a Mexican holiday or a possible fiesta. The annual "blessing of the animals" in the Easter period draws crowds. On the evenings devoted to Las Posadas, during the Christmas season, the candlelight processions start at the Ávila House and are spectacular—with fun at the conclusion provided by blindfolded children trying to whack specially-made *piñatas*, the breaking of which causes candies and surprises to spill out on the street or into the hands of those who can catch them. On Sundays Mexican-Americans come from miles away to go to the old church and then to wander down Olvera Street.

The final working out of the program which had been sparked by "Save the Ávila House!" was the establishment of the Plaza area and ten blocks surrounding as a state historical monument. This happy consummation came as the result of the good ideas and work of Leo Carrillo of the State Park Commission, County Supervisor John Anson Ford, Judge McIntyre Faries, president of El Pueblo de Los Angeles; County Counsel Harold W. Kennedy, Sheriff Eugene W. Biscailuz, and a host of other devoted Angelenos. Under the terms of an agreement entered into in 1953 by the state, the county, and the city this substantial segment of old Pueblo lands has been or is being acquired by the state. Funds for the purchase or condemnation were contributed jointly by the state and by the county and city.

The development and maintenance of Pueblo de Los Angeles State Historical Monument is in the hands of people dedicated to the preservation and re-creation of much of Los Angeles' Pueblo days. The state operates through its Division of Beaches and Parks and the county and city (by agreement) through Los Angeles' Department of Recreation and Parks. Under these governmental bodies are the officials, appointees, and architects who carry out specific projects. The area of their planning and activities has Alameda Street for an easterly boundary and Ord Street for the most northerly. Arcadia Street—that is, the new Arcadia Street which adjoins the Hollywood Freeway—is the boundary on the southwest, while the most westerly limit is curving Hill Street just below the Pioneer Memorial with its paneled sculpture, waterfall, and greenery.

The plans for development are ambitious, are continuous, and are spread over at least a ten-year period. With due allowance for the right of government to change its mind or switch goals, the program calls for certain streets to be vacated, or closed, or rerouted; certain buildings to be torn down, others to be restored to their former glory; the approximate location of the original Plaza to be marked on the ground and to contain, possibly, the statue of Governor Felipe de Neve, the city's founder; with a bandstand to be placed in the center of the present Plaza where modern bands can remind listeners of Commodore Stockton's musicians who played there in 1846 and 1847. The restoration of the Pico House as a functioning hotel of the 1870s and 1880s through lease to a nationwide hotel chain and the bringing back to life of the Merced Thea-

Christine Sterling, reactivator
of Olvera Street and
managing director
El Pueblo de Los Angeles.

ter as a functioning show house of the same period (with the
co-operation of little theater groups) are perhaps the most
exciting of the projects. The Masonic Temple receives at-
tention, too, while the old Firehouse that faced the Plaza in
the 1880s and 1890s comes back with a horse-drawn fire-
wagon ready to gallop to a four-alarm fire. The Garnier Building on Sanchez Street, for half a century the headquarters of
the Chinese community, continues—in current planning—to
reflect the contributions of Chinese-Americans to Los Angeles, through exotic shops and a restaurant at least. Even the
church has a face-lifting to bring it in line with Pueblo days.
The Bank of America's reconstruction of the Simpson Building, which arose on the site of a Mexican gambling house of
the 1840s, into a Mexican-style *banco*, with Spanish-speaking
personnel, helps transform the Plaza into an actual Latin-
American center. Immediately adjoining the bank and a part
of the same building is a first-class Mexican grocery and tor-
tilla factory, greeting the entrants to Olvera Street. This is
supplemented by a Latin-American hospitality center and
consular headquarters and Inter-American library—also facing
the Plaza—which re-shapes and takes over much of the Methodist Headquarters Building which arose on the site of Judge
Olvera's home. Here Eugene W. Biscailuz has his office as vice
president in charge of Latin-American affairs for El Pueblo de
Los Angeles. Continuing to function is La Plaza Iglesia Meto-
dista. Close to the Plaza, the Ávila House receives the atten-
tion required for its preservation, along with the brick Pelanconi and Sepúlveda structures, also on Olvera Street. An in-
formation center, outdoor exhibits, plantings, parking, and

walkways are on the lengthening agenda. Even something that will recall to mind the Indians of Yang-na days is contemplated.

The Pueblo de Los Angeles State Historical Monument is a place of short, lively streets converging on the Plaza. On occasions it is thronged. Year by year, through the thoughtful activities of state, county, and city, it continues to help tell the story of the founding and evolution of a city that is now the nation's third in size. On-the-ground tours of the old Pueblo area, beginning with the Plaza, are fun. So, too, are those tours made sitting in an armchair—reading the story presented here and following the historical map with which it is supplemented. The map indicates the old streets and the sites of the adobe buildings which were the center of life and interest to *rancheros* and townsmen during the heyday of the old Pueblo. As the Pueblo de Los Angeles State Historical Monument through the years attains goals set for it, the Plaza comes to life and becomes increasingly exciting and significant.

Plaza Church, Los Angeles, in the 1870s, the happy conception of Albert J. Kramer, Los Angeles artist. Reproduced through the courtesy of Mr. Kramer, owner of the Painting.

Calendar of Events in the History of Los Angeles

1769   The first white visitors to the Los Angeles area—members of a party of Spanish explorers led by Gaspar de Portolá—name the river and comment on the excellence of the site for a settlement.

1771   Mission San Gabriel is established—the first white settlement in what is now Los Angeles County.

1781   On September 4, 1781, the Pueblo of Los Angeles is started as a farming community by a group of settlers recruited for that purpose in Sinaloa and Sonora villages of Mexico.

1784   The rancho period begins through the granting by Governor Fages of the first three land concessions within the Los Angeles County area. In time the Pueblo is surrounded by ranchos and becomes the social and trading center.

1818   Site chosen for Los Angeles' present Plaza and Church. The Church is dedicated in December of 1822.
Joseph Chapman leaves a coast-raiding party at Monterey, later to settle as a "regenerated pirate" in the Pueblo of Los Angeles—its first American and a most useful citizen.

1822   The Spanish regime in Alta California gives way to Mexican rule. In Los Angeles the *ayuntamiento* or council form of city government is fully established.

1835   The status of Los Angeles is raised to that of a city *(ciudad)*.

1845   Los Angeles is made the capital of Alta California.

1846-7   War between the United States and Mexico.

1848   California is ceded to the United States through the Treaty of Guadalupe Hidalgo.

1849   First survey of Los Angeles is made by Lieutenant E. O. C. Ord.

1850   Los Angeles is incorporated and the city and county governments organized under laws passed by the first American legislature. Population of Los Angeles city and county: 8329.

1856   Los Angeles' title to four square leagues of land, derived under Spanish laws governing pueblos, is confirmed by the United States Land Commission.

1857   Collapse of the boom in Southern California that had been started by the enormous demand for beef cattle from Gold Rush miners.

1860s   Break-up of the ranchos and the beginning of the agricultural era, including the commercial planting of orange groves.

1876   The coming of the railroad to Los Angeles and the end of its isolation, making possible the later waves of immigration.

1887-8   A real estate boom establishes much of the present pattern of cities in Los Angeles County.

1892   Discovery of oil in Los Angeles by E. L. Doheny.

1909   San Pedro Harbor becomes Los Angeles Harbor through the consolidation with Los Angeles of San Pedro and Wilmington —following the Shoestring Annexation of 1906 which had given Los Angeles a toehold on the ocean.

1910   Hollywood is annexed to Los Angeles—and in the years immediately following it becomes the world center for the making of motion pictures.

1913   Los Angeles begins to import water—first from Owens Valley; later from Mono Basin; and still later, in 1941, from the Colorado River.

1939   A union railroad station is completed.

1941-45 The industrial phase of Los Angeles' history begins as a part of World War II activities. With industrialization have come more people, more automobiles, smog—first noted in 1943; vast freeway development; and huge expansion of aerial travel. By 1959 the population exceeds 2,400,000.

1953   The city, the county, and the state agree to acquire in the state's name the Plaza and surrounding areas and to establish a state historical monument.

Concerning the print reproduced on the back cover

Los Angeles as it looked in 1857 to two San Francisco artists, Charles C. Kuchel and Emil Dresel, is shown in the print reproduced on the back cover. Lithographic prints, now collectors' items, were made from their drawings by Joseph Britton and J. J. Rey. Los Angeles, the adobe village pictured here in rich and illuminating detail—and with color now added by Irene Robinson—was the social and trading center of the ranchos during California's pastoral period. In 1857 it was still feeling the effects of the boom that filled rancheros' pockets with the gold paid for the cattle they drove north to satisfy the demands of Gold Rush miners. Main Street, on the left, stretches north toward the Plaza in this unique picture; Los Angeles Street, with its long row of merchants' shops, is on the right. Today, when the giant of Los Angeles has arisen and is in full stride—with its teeming population, its traffic, and its industrialism—it is good to take thought of the simple pueblo of a hundred and more years ago. (Courtesy Title Insurance and Trust Company.)

Los Angeles, 1857